William A. Redding

Mysteries unveiled

The Hoary Past comes forward with Astonishing Messages for the Prophetic Future

William A. Redding

Mysteries unveiled

The Hoary Past comes forward with Astonishing Messages for the Prophetic Future

ISBN/EAN: 9783337372132

Printed in Europe, USA, Canada, Australia, Japan

Cover: Foto ©Thomas Meinert / pixelio.de

More available books at **www.hansebooks.com**

No. 9

MYSTERIES UNVEILED

The Hoary Past Comes Forward with Astonishing Messages for the Prophetic Future

BY
WILLIAM A. REDDING

Copyright, 1896, by Wm. A. Redding
British and other foreign publishers are requested to honor the integrity of this copyright

PRICE: Paper Cover, 50 Cents; Cloth, $1.00

A STATEMENT.

In placing this book before the public it is not claimed that all the facts and thoughts in it are new, as Solomon says that there is nothing new under the sun, and I believe him. It is true that we are constantly meeting with things which we have never seen or heard before, but that is no proof that they were not in existence long before we met them. Principles *always* existed, but they lie dormant and unknown until some one comes along and, by revelation from some unseen force, discovers a point or two about them, and he applies them to use, and then the world declares that Mr. —— *"invented"* a great thing, whereas the fact is he *"invented"* nothing. He simply *discovered* a thing which had been in existence ever since God was in existence. It would have been just as easy to have steam engines, bicycles, printing presses, sewing machines, etc., etc., 6,000 years ago, when Adam was on earth, as it is to-day. The same principles were in existence then as now, but mankind did not know it; therefore, men have not *"invented"* any thing. And when they first catch the thought or light about these unknown principles, it is only a mere speck on one particular point, and when they put that point into operation more light comes to them about other principles connected with it; and thus it goes, on and on, higher and higher, towards perfection—gaining a little here and a little there. So much is being said on every line of thought nowadays that it is almost impossible to write upon any subject without running upon a part of some other person's thoughts, as *no one* man has discovered all that is known about any thing. It is like the fine machinery we have in the world to-day. One man discovered the principle of some part of it and this started another man's mind to thinking over it, so that he would see a new point which had never entered the mind of the first man; and thus it would go from one person to another, each adding on a new discovery until, finally, the machine comes out to-day a marvel of intelligence. Take the great Pyramid of Egypt, for instance, as a subject. Lawyers, doctors, preachers, editors, astronomers, college professors, judges and a great *host* of persons have been figuring on this great stone building many centuries—especially so during the last forty years. One person discovered that the Pyramid taught astronomy; another one found that it laid down a perfect system of weights and measures for man's use. Another saw the science of geometry and trigonometry set in it; and, finally, Mr. Robert Menzies, of Scotland, caught the idea that each inch represents a year, and that it had something to do with the Bible teaching; then Mr. C. T. Russell, of Pennsylvania, U. S., thought he saw the plan of the ages laid out in it, and he wrote a chapter about it and added on new points, and I have used many of his points and thoughts (rearranged) in my chapter about it and have added links which other writers had overlooked. Another, has written about the Pyramid and Freemasonry. Thus it goes from one to another. Stacks of money and much time have been expended in investigating it. Great societies in Europe and also here in America have been formed to study it. It has been the wonder of earth. Like a foot-ball, it has been kicked at from all sides to sound it. The prophets Isaiah and Jeremiah knew its greatness and spoke of it 2,500 years ago. So it is out of order for any *one* man to claim that he is the originator of all the ideas now put forth about the Pyramid or any other thing.

                                                          THE AUTHOR.

August, 1896.

TRACING THE THREAD.

The world has spiritualized every thing in the Bible to such an extent that it is looked upon as a sky book entirely—not having anything to do with this earth; and, as a consequence, it has lost its charm and worth in the minds of the people, as they regard it as an extremely foreign document, belonging to a far-off and high-up world, and hence its narratives are not interesting (to *their* minds) and, in most cases, not even believed as *realities*, but are regarded as mere fiction, manufactured by some unknown persons to make a plausible story. The constant spiritualizing of every thing has paralyzed the statements in the Book so that they fall flat without even a notice. But few people seem to know that the cities, rivers, mountains and countries mentioned in the Bible are located on this earth; and when we take up our Bible and commence to read and have our geographies and histories lying open by our side so as to trace as we read, the world stands astonished to think that the Book is talking about movements here on earth. They thought it was gabbling about the sky where there could be no hope of ever locating the places mentioned. So long as a person is ignorant of the exact location of the cities, rivers, mountains, countries, etc., mentioned in it and the dates when occurrences took place, he can not follow the thread of the narratives, and, of course, he loses interest in them at once—especially so if he attends the Sunday-schools and churches of to-day, as they always give the Book and its subjects a *far-off touch* and leave the impression that it contains much which was not intended for us to know. Their preacher has often talked about the River Jordan but always left them under the impression that it was that imaginary line between this life and the life "over there," after death. I never shall forget how delighted I was (several years ago) when I first learned that the same River of Jordan as mentioned in the Bible is in existence, here on this earth, and that it starts up in the Lebanon mountains, in the north end of Palestine, and runs south through the Galilee country and empties into the Dead Sea, which is some miles southeast of Jerusalem. Of course I had studied geography and various other things in school and was a school teacher in my younger days, and yet I was *intensely* ignorant on all Bible subjects. I knew nothing *at all* on that line and did not *want* to know any thing about it, as I had the idea that the Bible and its talk had nothing to do with *this* earth, but that it dealt entirely with dead persons, and as I was not dead I cared nothing about it. That is, I *thought* I was not dead; but I see *now* that I *was* dead, although I was walking around and talking like other people. I meet many dead persons nowadays walking around and arguing that it is the Tariff, or the Gold Standard or the Free Coinage or the Republican or Democratic or Populist parties or some foreign country that is causing all this uproar on the earth; and that their crop failed last year because it *"happened"* to be too dry or too many floods or that the cyclone took them or some other thing *"happened"* to strike. Such persons are dead. They know not any thing. They see not that the day of the world's trouble, mentioned by Jesus, is now here. They think the Bible is all sky and that it applies to them after they are buried. They see not the great fact that the Bible contains a record of the movements which the various nations and individuals are to make on this earth in coming to perfection, which is God. Nothing but a terrible grinding (already starting) will make them see this fact and wake them up out of their sleep of death, so that they can see that the great day of the battle of God Almighty is commenced. The sayings of Jesus to the young man are now clear. He said to him, "Follow Me." The young man replied, "Let me go back and bury my father, who is dead." Jesus said, "Let the dead bury the dead." Jesus, with His wonderful illumination, knew that the people were all dead and had no *Life* or knowledge in them, and that they could attend to burying that boy's father, who was simply colder and less active than the others around him. They were all dead together and knew not any thing. That saying of Jesus about the dead burying the dead always looked to me as being foolish and extremely absurd until I came out of darkness into light so that I could see how intensely dead the people are and how decidedly wrong they regard the Bible and its teachings. Church-members and all others (except the spiritually illuminated) are just the same. They are all dead together and are waiting for burial. Their idea is that they must be buried and go away "over there" in order to see the Lord, not seeing the startling fact that the Lord is here and that the kingdom of God is within us; and if the kingdom is *within* us, then it is plain that the King resides in His kingdom. The president of the United States does not reside in Germany; neither does the czar of Russia reside in England. They live and have their habitation in their own governments, where they belong.

If I want to see the president of the United States I certainly will not leave this land and go off to another country to find him. Up to this time the teaching has always been pointing us to the "over there" beyond the grave, and holding out the idea that it is impossible to speak with God or know Him until we arrive at that far-off country. This puts the Lord and the Bible and all our good time away off and uninteresting; and I am writing this book and digging up the ancient things and locating places and giving dates, etc., to *force* your mind to see that the King rides up and down through the earth and handles the nations and individuals and turns governments up or down to suit His own purposes. You must know that the redemption of mankind is to take place *here on earth*, and that it is already commenced with great force and velocity while dead men are walking around arguing that it is the Tariff or Free Trade or paper money or some other imaginary thing that is washing our foundation from under us. They see not that it is the River of Life turned on and that it is running through and around the Tree of Life and washing the rubbish away. The Bible tells us that the Tree of Life is to be in the center of the River of Life and also on both sides of it so that the water runs through it. Rev. 22:1-6. The Tree of Life is mankind planted in the center of God with His powerful Spirit running through and around them; therefore, the trashy stuff now piled up around men and nations is being torn away by the irresistible River. Jesus was in the middle of this River, and this is why He said "The Father is in Me and I am in the Father." All willing mankind is (eventually) to come into the middle of this River, here on earth; and by producing facts, figures, dates and places I hope to break your false ideas about wanting to be buried and go away to see God when God is here. A very little circumstance, sometimes, starts the mind on a new line of thought. For instance, some years ago I picked up a little book that was thrown around, and, as I always examine every thing, I began to read it and found that it was a sort of comment on the general character of the Jordan River, etc. Facts and figures were set forth which made it plain to my mind that it was the *real* river mentioned in the Bible. New light flashed across my mind, and I felt that I had discovered a great fact. The idea that the Bible occurrences had a foundation on this earth brought the Book closer home to me and I then began to think about it and look into it; and I have gone on, from one thing to another, until I find that it is a home Book entirely. This is why I have so much to say in my publications about the *tribes*, nations and different peoples. I know that if persons can be disentangled on all these things they will see the Bible in a new light which brings it closer home to them so that they can take it into their minds and comprehend the movements of God, as He handles the nations and turns governments up or down and changes the affairs of earth. It is an astonishing study and will show that every thing goes on like clock-work, with each wheel turning around in its place to produce its share of the work in the general outcome. Some of the wheels revolve rapidly and keep up a great friction and clatter, while others go very slow and unnoticable. These *seemingly* greatly mixed movements cause the people to think that the world drifts on in a haphazard way without management or order; but let me tell you that a *careful* tracing of things down the ages shows positive and perfect order and purposes knit together in the smoothest way. When their time comes they are there present, ready to drop into the notch made for them, and there is no such a thing as preventing them. You can catch hold of a spoke in the wheel and push backward, but it will run over you and sweep you down. But if you have sufficient foresight to see what is the matter and what a certain movement means, and if you will then take hold and urge it on you thereby put yourself in the current of spiritual force hovering around that movement, and you become not only enlightened but powerful. But you must be *certain* that you understand the purpose of God and take His side of the case; and in making up your mind on this point you dare not judge by appearances, as it is scarcely ever, I might say *never* the smooth or best *looking* side that is God's side when viewing the great movements of nations, etc., for the reason that mankind is turned just half way around so that its face looks in an opposite direction from God and sees things with the map turned upside down; hence the movements and pictures on the right-hand side appear on the left and are standing on their heads, which looks to the deluded human eye as ridiculous; while the mixed and upside-down affairs of men on the left hand are given a correct appearance on account of being viewed from the wrong direction. It is the turning of men's faces around *right* that causes the uproar and clashing among them. They think evil is then striking them and they will fight the turning with a *vengeance* and do every thing in their power to defeat it, so as to be left in their old and upside-down condition. This is exactly the situation at this time throughout the earth—especially among the Anglo-Saxon nations (United States, Canada, England, etc.), where the great body of the Lost Ten Tribes of Israel reside, as the Lord chose *them* and set them apart as the *leaders* in the Millennial Kingdom which is now being prepared for the world, and therefore, the commotion attending the preparation naturally strikes more lively and noticeable among those people, as a complete change is to take place in the affairs of earth, and as *they* are to lead it, the stirring and breaking are greatest among them. We, the Lost Ten Tribes of Israel, were brought to England and to America and were given advantages for a purpose and we would better be fulfilling that purpose *immediately*.

<blockquote>
The Lord will set thee on high above all nations of the earth, and make thee the head and not the tail, and thou shalt be above and not beneath.—Deut. 28:1, 10, 13. The Lord hath chosen thee to be a special people unto himself above all other people that are upon the face of the earth. Thou shalt be blessed above all people.—Deut. 7:6-14. I am not sent but unto the lost sheep of the House of Israel (Lost Ten Tribes).—*Christ in Matt. 15:24.*
</blockquote>

Therefore, we being the people to whom He entrusted His doctrines, we would better right ourselves and not be caught napping or playing with *pretensions* in the form of present church creeds. We started in the Garden of Eden and have finally landed here in the United States for a purpose. We know just where we are located. We can find the spot on the map; therefore, let us hunt for our *starting* point. It is an actual spot of land on the earth, although most people think it was a sky location or a fictitious story manufactured to suit the occasion, and when we talk about hunting for the exact location of the Garden of Eden here on earth people open their eyes in astonishment. The Bible account of creation and of the Eden transaction makes no pretension of being *inspired*. It simply starts out and begins to tell things without saying who is telling them or *when* it occurred. It is generally believed that Moses wrote the first five books in the Old Testament; and we know that Moses was born *about* 1572 B. C. and that he resided the first 40 years of his life in Egypt, when he killed an Egyptian and had to run away and hide from the sheriff 40 years (see Exodus 2:11-16 and Ex. 4:18-20). This would make him 80 years old. He then returned to his old home and led the Twelve Tribes across the wilderness 40 years, which would make him 120 years old, and it is quite probable that he wrote the book of Genesis just before his death, which occurred when he was 120 years of age. This would make the date of the writing of Genesis 1452 B. C. And we know that Adam was created a little over 2,500 years before this period; therefore, the record of the creation of Adam and Eve was written 2,500 years *after* the occurrences took place; but it is just as easy for spiritual Wisdom to look backward and see what *has* occurred as to look forward and tell what *will* occur. And whoever wrote the first five books of the Old Testament was either inspired or else an extraordinary good guesser, as statements are there made about the divisions of the people and what the outcome would be in future that present facts verify as truth. This being the case, we have a reasonable right to examine the statements about locations and the transactions which took place before Genesis was written and we naturally begin at the Garden of Eden where Adam was planted, as it is generally believed that we are his descendants and, therefore, we go to the Garden for our starting point. "But where was it located?" you will ask. "Did it, as a spot of ground, ever really exist on earth?" I am forced to believe that it did. I am aware of the fact that persons are now teaching the idea that the Garden of Eden was not a section of country, but that it was a race or races of people in whom God worked out certain purposes; therefore, those people were the "garden." This, in *one* sense, is true, but there certainly was a particular location called the Garden of Eden, as the Bible mentions certain well known rivers as flowing out of the Garden and this indicates that it was a section of country. There is a tendency nowadays to symbolize every Bible statement and make it vanish into thin air so that there is nothing to it. There are a great host of people who believe or *pretend* to believe that no such a person as Jesus ever lived. They argue that it was simply a *principle* and was named Jesus, but that the *real* flesh man Jesus was not on earth. This shows how far people will carry a thing when once they start out to spiritualize every thing in the Bible. They do away with every man, city, river, mountain, sea, house, etc., etc., and declare that no such things existed, but that they were simply *principles* called by those names, and that the real things never existed. They declare that there was no Moses; no Twelve Tribes of Israel; no city of Jerusalem; no David; no Israel Kingdom; no Jesus; no twelve apostles; no real crucifixion of a man on a cross; no prophet Daniel; no anything. They say that none of these things existed, although the discoveries of to-day are digging up old bricks and pottery with names and dates; and recently some old gates were dug up in Jerusalem, after having been buried nearly forty feet deep some 3,000 years. The

Bible talks about these gates, but our spiritualizing friends say that it was all "principles" and symbols and that no gate, no city, no man living in the city ever existed; but we dig up the gates just the same. I admit that nearly every thing which took place in ancient time *represented* some spiritual purpose, but it is the most absurd foolishness to say that the *actual* thing or occurrence never was on earth. Political parties strive over a certain principle. Each party has its candidate up, who is supposed to stand for or against that principle as they desire. The vote is taken on the *men*, with nothing said on the ticket about the principle, as that is understood. After the election is all over will any person pretend to say that the actual real flesh men, as candidates, never existed? All the Bible symbols were acted out by men, women, cities, etc., and it will not do to say that these agents of the symbols never existed, although there are people who are teaching just such foolishness, and it has a tendency to run Bible statements into a nothing, so that people regard the Bible as gabbling about the air in the sky. This is why I am writing a book of this kind. I want the people to see that the Bible deals with God's movements among men and governments. Jesus represented a grand spiritual principle. He *was* that principle, and He brought it to light. Jerusalem stood for a principle or was a symbol; but will any person make himself ridiculous by saying that the real flesh man Jesus and the real city of houses never existed? There is a tendency just now for the people to argue themselves and every thing else out of existence. No God; no world; no Jesus; no men. They leave every thing a great big blank, beyond all possibility of ever learning. Such trashy doctrine is destructive to men's moral and spiritual makeup. It is possible to become acquainted with God and talk with Him and He to talk with us and this will be done within the next few years. It is done now by a few persons scattered over the earth. But we must lay down every thing and ourselves too and give up to Him completely and then He will act as our King. Many of the *seeming* impossibilities are coming under our control already and many more will follow. The Garden of Eden has long been looked upon as a nothing. A mysterious figure of speech with no basis or foundation at any particular place, but the writer of Genesis describes characteristics about it that make it certain that it was located somewhere along the banks of the Euphrates river which rises at the foot of Mt. Ararat (in central Armenia) and zigzags southwest, south and southeast, 1,800 miles long, to the Persian Gulf. Now go along that river and look for *other* earmarks that belonged to the Garden, according to the record which reads as follows:

And a river went out of Eden to water the garden; and from thence it was parted and became into four heads. The name of the *first* is Pison, which compasseth the whole land of Havilah, where there is gold, bdellium and the onyx stone. (Remember this point.) The name of the second river is Gihon, which compasseth the whole land of Ethiopia. (Not Ethiopia of Africa, but of Asia.) The name of the third river is Hiddekel (the Tigris river), which goeth toward the east of Assyria. And the fourth river is Euphrates.— Gen. 2:10-15.

Therefore, by the above description we see that four great rivers are brought into the account of the Garden location. Can any such a spot, fitting the above description, be found on earth to-day? Yes. One of the rivers (Euphrates) is a *certainty*. The

Hiddekel (*now* called the Tigris river), "which goeth toward the east of Assyria," is *another* certainty. It runs into the Euphrates about 120 miles northwest of the Persian Gulf. So here are *two* of the great rivers joined together. Go down the Euphrates five miles further and another great river (the Kerkhah, 500 miles long) comes in from the northeast (rather north) where it has its head in the Elam country and near a broken chain of mountains where it is possible the gold, onyx-stone and bdellium were found as reported in the description quoted above in reference to the Pison river which was one of the four belonging to the Eden description. This Kerkhah river may be the Pison mentioned; and if such is the case, we have *three* of the rivers located. Go on down the Euphrates further and another large river (the Kuran river) comes in from the east or northeast. It may be the Gihon river which the Bible mentions as one of the four. The Bible says the Gihon ran clear through the land of Ethiopia. The word *Ethiopia* means *burnt faces* (black like sunburn); that is, the people were dark color. These people came from Cush, the eldest son of Ham (see Gen. 10:6); and Ham was one of the sons of Noah (see Gen. 10:1). And wheresoever these Cush people (black color) resided, the ancients designated that country the land of Cush. Cush means *black* and Ethiopia means *burnt faces* (dark) and hence the country would be called Ethiopia (burnt faces) or Cush (black faces). For this reason (black color) three countries, in ancient times, were called Ethiopia or land of Cush. One of these Cush (Ethiopia) countries joined the Persian Gulf on the north and extended northward along the Tigris river in Persia, to Media, which is south of the Caspian Sea. The river Kerkhah, heretofore discussed as possibly the ancient Pison river, runs clear through this Cush country. The Bible tells us that the Pison river ran clear through the land of Havilah where there is gold, onyx-stone, etc. *Havilah* was one of the sons of Cush. See Gen. 10:7. In ancient times the country was named after or for the leading man or race occupying it, and it is quite likely that Havilah lived near or in the vicinity of his father, Cush, and therefore Havilah and his descendants had a tract of country named Havilah near or in or joining the land of Cush. This would account for the Bible record which says that the Pison river ran through the land of Havilah and that the Gihon river ran through the land of Ethiopia (meaning burnt faces), which, as I have shown, is the same as Cush, which means black. Therefore, it is not hard to understand how these names are associated with each other, Havilah being the son of Cush and Cush being black, which brings th same result as Ethiopia, which means burnt faces. Therefore, the Pison river could run through the Havilah country, while the Gihon river could run through the Ethiopia country, which is the same as the Cush country. This would put one river in the land of Cush, the father, while the other river would be in the land of Havilah, the son. This could be possible with the two rivers (the Kerkhah and the Kuran) which I have named as possibly the Pison and the Gihon connected with the Garden of Eden description, as the Kerkhah and the Kuran both run through the Cush country; and if it was divided between the father's descendants (Cushites) and the son's descendants (Havilahites) it is reasonable to think one river was in the Havilah land and the other river in the Cush (Ethiopia) land; and we have Bible evidence that this Cush country lay north and northwest of the Persian Gulf in Persia, Asia, and that it was traversed by rivers. See Zeph. 3:10. Isa. 11:11. Ezek. 38:5. Here then we have four rivers which fulfill, reasonably well, the description laid down in the Bible about the Garden of Eden; and *two* of these rivers (the Euphrates and the Tigris) are counted certainties, as the *Euphrates* is named outright as *one* and the Tigris is called Hiddekel "which goeth towards the east of Assyria," and this just fits the description of the Tigris. And we know that the land of Cush in Asia was on the north coast of the Persian Gulf, just where all these rivers have their way; therefore, we have the Garden of Eden run down to a close quarter on earth. We have the Euphrates and the Tigris rivers as certainties; and two other rivers which fit, reasonably well, the description laid down in Genesis 2:11, 13. We have the land of Havilah and the land of Ethiopia or Cush; but as to this (the land of Ethiopia) you are not to get the idea that it is the Ethiopia in Africa. That, in Africa, is an entirely different tract of country which was also occupied by Cush and his descendants. It is now called Abyssinia, Nubia and Sennaar. These tracts lie south of Egypt in Africa; but this is not the Ethiopia mentioned in connection with the Garden of Eden. It seems that there were three tracts of country occupied by the Cush (black) descendants, and each tract or vicinity was called Ethiopia (burnt faces). One of these places was in Africa, as just described, while the other two neighborhoods were in Asia; and we know that *one* of them in Asia was on the north coast of the Persian Gulf in the vicinity of the four rivers just named.

There is another spot in Asia where the Garden of Eden *may* have been located. At the head of the Euphrates river, up in Armenia, is a place where four great rivers rise within a few miles of each other. The Euphrates, Tigris, Araxes and the Phasis. The first two flow southward into the Persian Gulf, while the Araxes flows northeast into the Caspian Sea, while the Phasis flows northwest into the Black Sea. The Araxes and the Phasis may have been the Pison and the Gihon. Here, within a small area are the heads of four great rivers, the Euphrates and the Tigris being *two* of them and which I have heretofore shown are certainties that belonged to the Garden according to the Bible account.

The spot of country where the four rivers (in Armenia) rise is yet a beautiful location, just west of Mt. Ararat where Noah's Ark rested after the Flood. This fact is circumstantial evidence that Adam's race lived near there, as it is not probable that the Ark floated away far from where it started. But there is one objection to this spot as the Eden. It is (*now* at least) rather cold there. Snow covers Mt. Ararat all the time; and the climate is not so well adapted to Adam and Eve's fig-leaf clothing as the north coast of the Persian Gulf (heretofore described as the probable Eden spot) would be. However, we can not form conclusions from this standpoint, as the changes in the lay of the country, produced by the Flood, *might* have changed climatic conditions also. But it is reasonably certain that the Garden of Eden was located at or near one or the other of these two places. One was at or near the *mouth* of the Euphrates river, where four great rivers come together; while the other spot is at the *head* of the Euphrates where three other rivers rise and start out in different directions.

> And a river went out of Eden to water the garden; and from thence it was parted, and became into four heads.—Gen. 2:10.

This reading hardly fits the Armenia spot near Mt. Ararat, as these (the four) rivers rise in a tract of country and start out in different directions so that their mouths are many hundreds of miles apart. The Bible description does not say that the rivers *parted* into four *mouths*, but it says that *a* river went out of Eden and from thence parted into four *heads*. From this it would be necessary for the Garden to be on the main river at a point near where the other three rivers came together and joined the Garden river. The mouths of these rivers would be together or near each other, but their four heads would be widely apart and located in different directions. This greatly favors the idea that the Garden was on the Euphrates, northwest of the Persian Gulf, where the Cush (Ethiopia in Asia) and the Havilah land was, as heretofore shown. Therefore, having found, pretty closely, the place where the Adam people started, let us briefly trace the thread to its main places, leaving out all the minor points, and note the peculiar circumstances which would arise to scatter and drive the people to different parts of earth. The first notable occurrence of this kind was when they conceived the idea that they would build a high monument (called the Tower of Babel) to perpetuate their name.

> And the whole earth was of one language and of one speech. And as they journeyed from the east they found a plain in the land of Shinar and they dwelt there. And they said one to another, Let us build a city and a tower and make us a name, lest we be scattered abroad upon the face of the earth.—Gen. 11:1-5.

After the Flood the descendants of Noah located in the rich valley in Shinar along the Euphrates river, northwest of the Persian Gulf, and intended to concentrate themselves there into a close settlement and stay on that one spot of earth and build up great improvements to perpetuate their name. All this was contrary to the divine plan, as it would leave the remainder of earth not populated; therefore, after the people had commenced their great monument (Tower of Babel) the Lord confused their language so that one could not understand the other, and of course their associations were decidedly uninteresting to each other, and they divided off into little squads—each of which contained, probably, only such persons as could speak and understand the language of that squad.

And the Lord said, Behold, the people are one and they have all one language; let us go down and confound their language, that they may not understand one another's speech. So the Lord scattered them abroad from thence upon the face of the earth.—Gen. 11:6-8.

It would be natural for them then to seek a location, each squad to itself; and to do this they would scatter out and hunt up a location for each colony. This is just what the Lord wanted, so that the earth would be populated. A careful tracking of these movements shows that as the time would come for a new section of country to be settled some circumstance would arise to divide the people in opinion so that one part would pull out and hunt up a new location. It is highly interesting to run over history and notice how mysteriously these things have occurred. After the Noah descendants were scattered, one of them (Abraham) was chosen by the Lord to be the head or commencement of a special nation of people to lead in things godly, and, of course, they had to be specially taught and, therefore, they were separated from other people right from the start, beginning with Abraham. He resided at Ur (on or near the Euphrates river) in Mesopotamia, several hundred miles north (and a little east) of Jerusalem. The Lord commanded him to leave his kindred and his old home and go southward into Palestine.

The Lord said unto Abram, Get thee out of thy country (Mesopotamia) and from thy kindred and from thy father's house unto a land that I will shew thee, and I will make thee a great nation and I will bless thee and make thy name great, and in thee shall all families of the earth be blessed. And Abram took Sarah his wife * * * and they went forth to go into the land of Canaan (Palestine), and into Canaan they came.—Gen. 12:1-6.

They and their descendants lived in Canaan until their *allotted time* came to go Egypt, as God had told Abraham that his descendants would be driven to a strange land not belonging to them, and that they would stay in the strange land 400 years and be servants or slaves.

And he (God) said unto Abram, Know of a surety that thy seed shall be a stranger in a land not theirs: and they (the Egyptians) shall afflict them 400 years.—Gen. 15:13.

A famine in Palestine (at the proper *time*) forced them to move to Egypt (in Africa) as this was the "strange land" mentioned by the Lord and they *did* stay there 400 years (from 1900 B. C. to 1500 B. C.) and towards the expiration of that time the kings of Egypt became so extremely pinching on them that they could hardly live there. Their time had come for them to move out of Egypt to Palestine which was ready for them, and Moses was down in the desert (alone) taking lessons in the spiritual school of God so as to be ready to lead the Israelites out when their last hour had expired for them to be there. They were grumbling and growling about the "hard times," but never even suspicioned that God had the man (Moses) who was to lead them out down in the desert teaching him how to be a great captain over them and speak the commands of God to them. They thought a great evil had struck them in Egypt. They did not know that by moving out from there and going to Palestine they could have a government of their own with God (in the prophets) talking with them. Their condition was to be *bettered* instead of being made worse, but they could not see that point, even though God had their leader (Moses) away preparing him for the move then. They moved over into Palestine and were established into a government of their own, but when the time came for a change in their affairs a difficulty arose among themselves and general dissatisfaction set in and grew worse and worse many years.

Their kingdom had run its course and had come to its jumping-off place. God *permitted* the kings, one after another, to act in what *we* would call an unreasonable manner. They were hard and cruel on the people and over-taxed them and burdened them down in every way, and the more the people complained the harder the king burdened them, until finally a majority of the people rose up and left the government and scattered out to some other point and set up a new thing. It is positively stated in 1 Kings 12:1-25 and 1 Kings 11:31-36 and Zech. 11:14 that God caused the division of the Israelitish kingdom. He had a purpose in it. Zech. 11:14 says He wanted to break the brotherhood between Israel (Ten Tribes) and Judah (Jews). The *purpose* is not stated, but by looking back at the movements which have taken place *since* then we can get a little hint as to what *some* of the purpose was. England and all Europe were lying there west of them needing these people to develop the resources of the land and at the same time spread the godly instructions which they had received many hundreds of years through Moses and the prophets. They finally drifted over that way and things went well and flourishing for a time until their time came to "move on," then religious bigotry and oppression set in upon them and became so galling that they looked for a new location where they could worship God in their own way without dictation. Here was all this rich North American country lying idle with every thing favorable in it for spiritual development and His chosen family of Israel well started in spiritual schooling. It seemed proper to bring these people and this country together, and circumstances arose that accomplished it, and the result is, we find here in the United States the most advanced spiritual people—a select number of whom are to lead in the Millennial Kingdom and act as the "governors of Judah." Zech. 12:6.

After settling in America things went on in a flourishing way a few hundred years until about all of the desirable parts were settled and then a condition arose that gradually agitated the people to discontentment; and a disrupted condition will be the result, just as each change has brought during the last 6,000 years. Before the change occurred in Egypt the rulers (Pharaohs) bound them down harder and more severe until they became discontented and *willing* to leave. In Palestine the same thing occurred. In England the oppression took on more of a religious turn. They were persecuted and forced to a certain religious belief until the situation became a burden. Now the oppression is of a financial, social and political nature, just as it was in Egypt from 1900 B. C. to 1500 B. C. and in Palestine from 1025 B. C. to 975 B. C., which was 50 years of oppression and stubborn rulers who lashed the people right and left with tasks, taxes and trouble until they rose up and broke the kingdom. See 1 Kings 11 and 12. These chapters show that the people here *now* are complaining of the same things which disturbed and split the Israel kingdom 975 B. C.; and the Bible *positively* declares that God did it. You see their time had come for dissolution and scattering. The same smothered upheaval is growing among us *now* as grew between us 975 B. C. *Exactly the same.* People now are cursing their rulers, and the more they curse and froth the more contrary and pinching the rulers become. You see our *time* for dissolution and disruption is nearly here. A new thing is to be started up again. Palestine and Jerusalem are being cleared out and lifted up for us again. There they lie waiting for us to come back.

O, ye mountains of Israel, ye shall shoot forth your branches and yield your fruit to my people of Israel, for they are at hand to come. I am for you and I will turn unto you (Palestine) and ye shall be tilled and sown; and I will multiply men upon you—all the House of Israel.—Ezek. 36:8-13.

Every thing goes on *time*, and when the *time* comes for breaking up the old order of things and scattering and collecting to a new spot on earth the *causes* that will produce it begin to set in and grow up to such proportion as to rift every thing open; and this is the sole and only cause of the present disrupted condition of politics, churches and society. Our *time* has come and nothing can put it down or prevent it. You might as well try to lasso the moon. It will plow right on through the clouds undisturbed while you pound the air and curse at the pinched condition of things and blame this ruler and that ruler, etc., etc. But you are not to draw from this that I advocate that God works evil. God is Love and doeth no evil, but His movements often *seem* to the human intellect as evil. No doubt Noah's descendants thought that a great evil had struck them when the confusion of tongues fell upon them and made their associations unpleasant—so much so that they gave up their old home and left, to other parts of earth. The Israelites thought a great evil had struck them when things became so pinching that they could not live in Egypt and had to move out; and afterwards they had to rebel against the king at Jerusalem and split the government in two. The Twelve Tribes had been living together about 1,000 years, and then to have a disruption and family quarrel seemed *bad* indeed, but God in His book (the Bible) says, "This thing is from *Me*." 1 Kings 12:16-25. Zech. 11:14. The Bible positively declares that God confused the tongues at the Tower of Babel and scattered the people. Gen. 11:1-10. The Bible tells us that God caused Nebuchadnezzar, king of Babylon, to come over to Jerusalem and break up and carry away the Jewish kingdom. Jer. 25. Of course the Jews thought a great evil had struck them.

People want to hold on to the *old* way. They can not see the good being prepared for them. Those who are to lead the New Nation are now in the spiritual school of God, as Moses was, and the great movement will occur ere long after things become more and more pinching. Mankind is so constituted that it has to be pressed and broken almost into atoms to wake it up to a sense of duty. Give men good health, a good bed in which to sleep and plenty to eat and they care nothing for God, spiritual things or any body. You can not even get their attention to listen to any thing spiritual. Talk on the subject makes them angry. It is only when they are sick or distressed in other ways and can not get relief that they are even willing to hear about the Good or the Unseen. This is *one* of the reasons why such terible oppression and disruptions have to come to create dissatisfaction and make them *willing* to let go the old and hear about the new; but breaking them loose from the old way is looked upon by them as evil striking them. Viewing things from *this* standpoint makes us look at some peculiar expressions in the Bible, in which it is *positively* declared that God creates evil.

> I form the light and create darkness. I make peace and create evil. I, the Lord, do all these things.—Isaiah 45:7. Shall there be evil in a city and the Lord hath not done it?—Amos 3:6.

The above scripture, if properly translated, has some meaning, but I am satisfied that mankind (at present) is not fit to pass judgment on the question, as people always look at things from a *human* standpoint which is *always* wrong and short-sighted.

> *For my thoughts are not your thoughts, neither are your ways my ways, saith the Lord. For as the heavens are higher than the earth, so are my ways higher than your ways and my thoughts higher than your thoughts.*—Isaiah 55:8-9.

The people are complaining and fearful that the

present system of governments, churches and society will perish, as it is being paralyzed now before their eyes and they think they would be ruined if the present order of things were taken away from them. They can not see that a better thing—the *best* thing that was ever established on this earth for mankind is to take the place of the present unsatisfactory condition. They look at all this breaking up now as evil. In the springtime the warm atmosphere causes the ice in the rivers to break loose, and the pieces rear and plunge and roll over each other and sweep away bridges and every thing before it. It is destructive. You must keep out of its way. Within *itself* it is a highwayman, full of slaughter; but what caused it? What is coming *behind* it? Growth, beauty and bountifulness. The grass, the leaves on the trees, the fine fruit, the grain and bountiful crops are coming along *immediately behind* all the slaughter and madness. They could not have come had the ice remained frozen and hard. It had to give way first; and the same atmospheric conditions that caused the ice to rise up and strike at things brought the grass and the golden grain. We are just now coming to the golden harvest of all *past* ages. The great climax of perfection is *about* to commence and the same spiritual conditions overhead that are bringing it are also breaking up the long frozen, icy condition that has held things down on the beastly plane 6,000 years. This breaking up is already causing suffering and slaughter to every thing in its way, just as the ice in the rivers does in its springtime breaking. Climb out of the way and hinder it not if you would not be destroyed by it. It is coming with *irresistible* force. Stand still and watch the redemption of Man and the earth, and see the rising of the New Nation that is to lead the world. Drop the foolish habit of *spiritualizing* every thing in the Bible and putting every thing away "up there," out of your reach. God is within you.

BRIEF EXPLANATION ABOUT THE GREAT PYRAMID OF EGYPT.

Before a person can fully understand the description of a piece of workmanship the plan of it must be thoroughly imprinted on the mind; therefore, it is necessary that you read this carefully and trace it on the diagram set in this book.

The Pyramid covers 13½ square acres and is 484 feet high.

Entrance 50 feet above ground and 25 feet east of center. Entrance door 47.3 inches high and 41.5 inches wide.

The Pit is 46 feet long and 28 feet broad, and is located 100 feet below the center of the base of the Pyramid.

Mosaic Hall is 47 inches high (to ceiling) and 41 inches wide and slants 26 degrees.

Floor length of Christian Hall, 1881.2 inches. Ceiling nearly 28 feet high. Door leading into hall, 53 inches high. Door leading out at top end of hall, 43½ inches. Short passage from top end of Christian Hall to Ante-Chamber, 52.19 inches. Length of Ante-Chamber, 116.26 inches; width, 65; height, 149. King's Chamber length, 412 inches; width, 206; height, 230. Temperature, 50 degrees. 180 feet of solid masonry between it and outside air; and 50 courses of masonry from base of Pyramid to this chamber. The stone box inside of it, and which is *supposed* to represent the Ark of the Covenant, is 89.62 inches long, 38.61 wide and 41.13 deep.

Age of Pyramid something over 4,000 years. Built about 300 years after Noah's Flood, according to the best calculations that can be found, although nothing positively certain can be stated on this point. It is largely conjecture, made up from mere circumstantial evidence. The ancient prophets seemed to have a knowledge of its meaning, as the following hints from them show:

> In that day shall there be an altar to the Lord in the land of Egypt and a *pillar* at the border thereof. And it shall be for a *sign* and for a *witness* unto the Lord.—Isaiah 19:19, 20.

> Ah Lord God! there is nothing too hard for Thee. The Lord of Hosts is His name, who has set *signs* and *wonders* in the land of Egypt, even unto this day.—Jeremiah 32.

You will notice that the above language of Isaiah says that there shall be a *pillar* at the border of Egypt for a "sign" and for a "witness" unto the Lord, but he carefully concealed what it was to "witness." The *time* had not come then for it to be understood and the prophets' words were veiled. And it is probable that much of its meaning is yet hidden from the minds of men. However this may be, it is a curious mystery and is hard evidence against a class of people who are now spiritualizing every thing in the Bible so that its statements are argued into thin air with no foundation under it, according to *their* teaching.

THE GREAT MYSTERY UNVEILED.

In the northern part of Africa stands the great wonder of the world. Generations have come and gone; they have looked and figured, guessed and studied with amazement—all to no purpose. The lock that sealed its lips, four thousand years ago, guarded carefully the hidden secrets in its care until the time would come for the voice within it to speak out to an astonished world. It has spoken, and all the earth stand in breathless amazement at its revelation. The veil is lifted sufficiently to expose *some* of its long-hidden treasures. Silent as the tomb at midnight it is, yet its great message rolls out upon us at an opportune moment when most needed. Its speechless oratory melts men down like sand. Well they may wonder in its presence, as Jehovah's tracks are there, but He covered them from the eyes of men, and sealed the wisdom of the ages in solid stone so that neither time nor the elements of weather can erase His secret path. Will you read this secret history? Come with me to the great Pyramid of Egypt—gray-headed with age. Take off your shoes and uncover your head in its towering presence, as Jehovah has been there. He was the architect whose plans and specifications were formed before the first morning stars sang together. He gave the orders and the foundation for this mysterious building was laid before the grandparents of Abraham were born. What is the measurement thereof? 764 feet square at its base and 486 feet high —covering about thirteen acres of ground. Built of stone laid solid within and without. Some of the stones being thirty feet in length and fit down upon each other so closely that the point of a pocket-knife blade can be run over them and not detect the joints —although no mortar was used in building. Where is the machinery to-day that will dress a 30-foot stone so accurately as to make such a joint? And the weight of such a stone! Some in the building are estimated to weigh 800 tons. What machinery can lift such a stone over 400 feet high and let it down so accurately as to make an almost unnoticeable joint? A common freight car will carry 20 tons; and at this rate it would require 40 cars to carry one stone. All the steam engines in the world could not pull this 13-acre building in one lump. Storms can not shake it, as it is solid through from side to side and from top to bottom except three or four little halls running through it at various angles; and in *these* some of the mysteries are built. It is shaped for strength—its four sides being tapered and slanted from its foundation upward until they all meet in a sharp point, 486 feet high; it is the very acme of wisdom in form and structure.

When was it built? What was the purpose? Who did the work? How many thousand men were engaged upon it? All these questions were asked thousands of years before Jesus was born. Away back in Jacob's time this great building troubled the heads of men, but *Jehovah* kept still; the time for unveiling its deep secrets had not yet come.

Who built it? It is not positively known, but *circumstantial* evidence seems to show that Melchizedek (the great peaceful king of Salem) managed the work; but he received the pattern, inside and outside, directly from God. The Bible mentions Melchizedek as having been a *type* of Christ—

that is, he was a great personage inspired by God. He lived about 2,000 or 2,500 years before Christ. Genesis 14:18,19 tells us that he was a priest of God and *blessed* Abraham; therefore, we know that Melchizedek was on earth at the beginning of Abraham's time. Abraham was born *about* 2021 B. C. How many thousand men worked on this great stone building? It is almost beyond the reach of human intellect to figure out an answer to this question. The stone had to be quarried and some of them hauled a long distance; and how this hauling was done, no human power can answer, as it has already been shown that one stone would weigh over 800 tons, and require 40 freight cars to carry it. The *dressing* of the stone would be an immense task. It could not be done by hand, as no workman nowadays can dress two stones (each thirty feet long) sufficiently true to make them lie together without showing the joint. Then the raising of an 800-ton stone into that high building and letting it down to its *exact* spot was a task which shows that the people of those days had ways and means unknown to us to-day.

How long time was consumed and what was the expense in erecting it? The Holy Ghost *only* can answer. If all the property in Egypt were sold the price would not be sufficient to hire workmen to tear down this great stone monument. The Designer (God) never intended that it should be torn down. It was to stand as a "witness" from generation to generation. It is the great hub of the world—standing in the center of all the land surface of earth. North and South America were not, at *that* time, known to exist and yet they were taken into consideration when the foundation spot was selected.

What was the *purpose* in building it? Ah, here is the great question that has been asked all through the ages, the last four thousand years, but never answered until the Lord was *ready* to let men into *some* of His secret plans. The prophet Daniel, writing under inspiration, declared that a time would come when "men would run to and fro and *knowledge* would be increased"; and sure enough that day is upon us and men are having their eyes opened on the mysteries of God and His universe. Railroad trains are carrying people to all parts of earth, and the scene at our great depots in large cities shows that the prophecies are now being fulfilled by people running to and fro—some going one way and some another. It is one continuous hurry and stir. Every body seems to be on the move. Trains, going in all directions, are crowded. People are discontented and want to be going; and if they can not go on railroads they go in wagons and on foot. Knowledge is being increased too. The Lord is dropping crumbs of wisdom into the minds of men as rapidly as they are willing to receive it, and this new current of force running through the thoughts creates fermentation while it is breaking people away from their old ideas, and this change causes a disturbed condition among the people; thus we see that the fulfillment of Daniel's prophecy is now going on; and with the increasing of knowledge, predicted by him, comes new knowledge about this great stone mystery in Egypt. The Lord has not permitted all its secrets to flow into *one* man; He has divided it among them by dropping a point to one and another point to another, and so on. The *first* discovery about it was that it contained scientific lessons in various lines of wisdom. It gives us the key to a correct system of weights and measures and to mathematical problems. It answers questions in astronomy. It points us to deep secrets in earth and sky. It shows the cycles or periods of revolution of the heavenly bodies. Its measurements and angles (when understood) point out the path of man and note the time when certain occurrences take place on earth. Although it was built more than two thousand years before Jesus Christ was born, yet it marks the exact date when that great event would occur. It shows His death and resurrection and the upward path of man towards perfection and notes the time when the Millennial Age will set in, and its great and final glory. It marks the calling of the Twelve Tribes of Israel and the wonderful dealings God has had with them and what is yet to occur. The path of all nations is shown and what their final destiny shall be. It shows the Holy and the Most Holy places, as they were pictured out before the Twelve Tribes of Israel during their celebrated journey of forty years in the wilderness. At *that* time the symbols were constructed of cloth and linen hung up to form chambers and ante-chambers, with curtains drawn between them; but in this great solid mystery in Egypt all these things and many more are shown in *stone.* Dates of occurrences are most ingeniously marked and yet not a picture, not a word, not a figure is to be found about it. The history and destiny of the world are carefully written in it and yet not a word is cut, painted or shown. It speaks in thundering tones to the ages, and yet its voice is silent as the grave. No human eye can read its astonishing story for the reason that no reading can be found there. Its wonderful messages never would be noticed by the sight, hearing, touch, taste or smell. These five senses of man are dumb in its presence. Jehovah has a way of concealing things and at the same time holding them up to full view.

None of the wicked shall understand, but the wise (spiritually wise) *shall understand.*—Daniel 12:10.

The great secrets and history dwelling in this Egyptian monument are brought to light by measurements and calculating its angles. If you know any thing about geometry and trigonometry you know that there is a way of measuring distances by a process called *triangulation*. Civil engineers use this method in figuring the distances across rivers or through mountains where the chain can not be carried. The rule works with exactness and shows distance more accurately than chain measurements; therefore, by applying this and other mathematical rules to the great stone Pyramid of Egypt it reveals wonders. It speaks out in thundering tones, and yet says not a word. For instance, by measuring the distance from its northeast corner (at base) to southwest corner, and adding it to the distance from northwest corner to southeast corner will show (in inches) the exact number of years in the precessional cycle (which is 25,827 years). The precessional cycle or period is the time required for the sun to make one revolution or circle around a central point, supposed to be Pleiades. Our earth and a great many other worlds circle around the sun. It is a center for them; but while they are whirling around the sun, the *sun* is moving in a large circle around Pleiades; and the time required to make this great circle is 25,827 years. Long before the wonders of the stone Pyramid of Egypt had been discovered, astronomers had figured out the time required for the sun to make this great journey, and their figures were the same as are now discovered in the Pyramid. Of course Jehovah knew all about the times and movements going on in the heavens and He secretly wrote them in this great stone building by making each inch count as one year; it is claimed therefore, when you want to know the length of time in any certain dispensation of God, or desire the date when a certain important event will occur, just pick up your tape-line and start around or through or over the Pyramid and note its measurements and angles and your question will be answered in inches or cubits.

Would you know the distance from this earth to the sun? Just measure the distance from the top point of the Pyramid to its base and note the slant of its sides and then apply the known rules of arithmetic, geometry and trigonometry in triangulation, heretofore mentioned, and your answer will be 91,840,270 miles as the distance between these two worlds. Long before the secrets of the Pyramid were unveiled astronomers had settled on the distance as 92 million miles, or thereabout. When the angles are given as a starting point, it is just as easy to calculate the distance from one world to another as it is to find the distance across a river without carrying the chain across the space, as triangulation rules are accurate, same as other mathematical rules; therefore, just lay your line on this stone Pyramid and your answer is sure. This is what the Bible is hinting at when it says:

Who hath laid the measures thereof and who hath stretched the line upon it?—Job 38:5.

God was asking Job certain mysterious questions to set Job to thinking about the wonderful things of the universe and the great wisdom required to construct them, and God used a building as a symbol to represent this earth, and asks the questions:

Where wast thou when I laid the foundation of the earth? Whereupon are the foundations thereof fastened? and who laid the corner stone thereof?—Job 38.

Investigation shows that the foundation for the Pyramid was carefully leveled on natural rock and a hole or socket cut down into the rock bottom, at each of the four foundation corners, so that the workmen could shape the first layer of dressed stone to fit into the sockets; representing by this that it should never slip off its foundation. The Lord was hinting to Job about these things.

Whereupon are the foundations thereof fastened? Who laid the corner stone thereof?

This stone Pyramid may be considered this earth built on a small scale and containing a full history of man and his winding path and the key to a system of weights and measures best adapted to man's use; and also marking the *hidden* dates when great changes or dispensations would set in, etc., etc.

The measurements of the four sides (at its base) added together gives the exact time in four years, to the very fraction—and makes due allowance for the leap-year.

There is but one opening into the Pyramid, and that is on the north side, and fifty feet above the base. From this entrance-door one starts into a narrow, straight, declining passage or hall-way, 4044 inches (337 feet) long. The slant is regular and rather steep and passes downward through the foundation of the Pyramid and goes on its downward course, through the natural rock, a distance of 100 feet below the base line until it meets a little room or "pit," 46x28 ft. cut in the solid natural rock *under* the Pyramid. As before stated, the distance from this "pit" room to the entrance door in the north side of Pyramid, is 4044 inches (337 feet). This is an important point to remember, as the length of this hall-way, expressed in inches, is supposed to give us the number of years the human race would be going down the slanting road towards the "pit" of trouble and disaster—counting from the time when the Pyramid was finished; now if we know when that building was completed we can start at that date and run down 4044 years and find when the time of trouble, spoken of by Christ and Bible writers, will begin. Their words on this turbulent time are as follows:

Wait, saith the Lord, until the day that I rise up to the prey, for my determination is to gather the nations to pour out upon them mine indignation.—Zeph. 3:8.

At that time there shall be a time of trouble such as never was since there was a nation.—Dan. 12:1.

For there shall be great tribulation, such as was not since the beginning of the world.—Matt. 24:21.

When was the Pyramid built? This is the point to be learned in order to get a starting point for the 4044 years. Ah, the date of the building of that great stone witness has troubled the heads of generations, but God had it marked in a hidden way so that when *"knowledge would be increased,"* as spoken of by Daniel, the Lord would let men into the important secret.

Mr. John Taylor, of England, was the first person to prove that the Pyramid was built for some good purpose, to teach mankind some lessons of importance, but his discoveries were all on the *scientific* branch of its teachings; and he published something about it in A. D. 1859. Since then many men have figured on it and written about it until many books and pamphlets on the subject are now in existence. Each man discovers some new point. Astronomers have been greatly interested in it for the reason that it teaches many things in their line. Prof. Piazzi Smyth, Astronomer Royal for Scotland, went to Egypt and made a study of it and took careful measurements of its angles and parts and made drawings of it—showing locations and lengths of halls and all the important points about it and wrote a book on it, entitled "Our Inheritance in The Great Pyramid." Part of the figures and drawings set out in this work are taken from his book. He was looking at it *entirely* from the basis of astronomy, without thinking that it had any thing to do with the Bible or God's plans; and while so engaged in figuring out the lessons in astronomy, as taught by the Pyramid, he noticed that the long, narrow slanting hall-way (entrance passage) resembled a telescope, pointing to a certain place in the heavens. He figured backward in astronomy to find when any planet had been at that spot in the sky; in other words, he turned the wheels of the universe backward until something would come in range with that hall-way in the Pyramid. He found that at midnight of the autumnal equinox, B. C. 2170, the *Dragon* star had been in direct line with the hall-way which points upward toward the *north*. There is another narrow hall leading off from the entrance hall and points upward towards the *south*. He figured backwards to find what planet would be in range with *it*, and he found that the cluster of seven stars called Pleiades was the object to which the *south*-pointing hall was calling on the night of autumn, B. C. 2170. He therefore concluded that the Pyramid was built (finished) 2170 B. C. After Prof. Smyth had discovered these lessons in astronomy, another gentleman named Robert Menzies caught the idea that the length of those halls had something to do with the mysteries of God's plan of the ages; and that by counting each inch as a year an astonishing message from God would be revealed. This new idea caused Prof. Smyth to do more measuring from a different starting point, to see whether the number of inches would tell when the pyramid was built. The entrance hall (starting in from the north side of the Pyramid) runs south and downward, as before stated, 4044 inches, but 628 inches from its starting point another hall sets in and runs upward 1,542 inches to where it meets and runs into a gallery whose ceiling is twenty-eight feet high from the floor of it. Mr. Menzies claimed that this high gallery was to represent the Christian Age, and that the point where the hall ceiling suddenly jumped up to such a great height was to represent the birth of Christ. Astronomer Smyth saw at once that if Menzies' theory was correct, then by starting at that high ceiling point and measuring downward 1,542 inches, to where the hall joined and ran into the entrance hall, and from there upward to the door on north side of the Pyramid the number of inches would express the date when the Pyramid was built. He had already figured it out by astronomy that certain planets were in range with those two halls in the autumn of 2170 B. C., and he took *that* as the date of building; now would the number of inches from that high ceiling point to the outside entrance door show the same figures? This was a breathless test, but if Menzies' theory was right the figures would correspond with those already produced by calculations in astronomy. The end of the measuring line was laid at the point where the high ceiling gallery set in (birth of Christ point) and stretched downward along the floor to the point where that hall joined or ran into the other hall, and the figures on the tape showed 1,542 inches to that junction point where the two halls met. By this they knew that they were already to a point 1,542 years before the birth of Christ, and they were yet far from the outside (entrance) door of the Pyramid; so they laid the line at the 1,542 mark (junction point of halls) and started upward, in the other hall, toward the outside doorway; and just as they arrived at the edge of the entrance door they noticed a finely ruled line on the wall of the hall, and the figures on the measuring line to that marked point on the wall showed 628 inches. They had gone 628 years farther away from the birth of Christ. They had already come down the other hall 1,542 years from Christ's birth, and by adding the 628 inches (years) to the 1,542 would give the number of inches from Christ's birth point to the ruled line on the wall at the edge of the door. 628 added to 1,542 makes 2,170—exactly the number which Prof. Smyth had found by calculations in astronomy. This was stunning proof that each inch in the hall-ways represents a year and that the stone Pyramid was built (finished) 2170 B. C. Abraham was born near that time, and the Lord *called* him to be the head or father of a special race of people through whom the Lord would work to raise the nations of earth to a higher plane of life and come into closer relations with God.

The Lord said to Abram, Get thee away from thy kindred and from thy father's house, and I will make of thee a great nation, and in thee all families of the earth shall be blessed.—Gen. 12:1-3.

Abraham had a son named Isaac. Isaac had a son named Jacob. Jacob had twelve sons who became the heads of the Twelve Tribes of Israel. These Twelve Tribes were the specially chosen race which was to work out God's purpose. They

THE TWELVE TRIBES OF ISRAEL MOVING.

They left Egypt, under the leadership of Moses, 1492 B. C., and arrived in Palestine 40 years later and took possession of the land set off to them. This was their *first* return. There is to be a *second* return, which is just now (1896) being prepared and will probably take place somewhere near 1915 A. D., when the Millennial Kingdom will be set up on this earth to rule the world.

lived among the Egyptians and other people until God told Moses to lead them out of Egypt and take them to Palestine where they could have a government of their own and live to themselves and not mix with other nations. This date when they cut loose from other nations is marked in the stone Pyramid by the hall-way branching off from the entrance hall at a point just 1,542 inches (years) before the birth-of Christ point which is shown further up the hall at a point where the high ceiling commences. But the branching off of the hall at 1,542 inches (years) before the birth-of-Christ point must not be taken as the time and point where the Israelites left Egypt, as they were set apart from other nations and especially called of God 430 years before they left Egypt. The setting apart was done when God called Abraham to leave his father's house and his country and his kindred and go to the land set apart for him by the Lord. This was *about* 1922 B. C., and 430 years of "sojournings" subtracted from this would make the time of leaving Egypt somewhere near 1492 B. C.; and this point must be remembered when reading hereafter in this book about the hall which I have named the *Mosaic Hall*, simply for *convenience* and *not* to mean that the hall started in when Moses started with the Israelites out of Egypt, as such an understanding would mislead as to dates and measurements. And just so with the *Christian* Hall further up in the Pyramid. I have simply *named* it to distinguish one from the other without giving figures and lengths of dispensations, as it confuses the reader to lay too many figures and complicated calculations before him all at once. The 1542-inch hall slants upward at a steep rate and its ceiling is only four feet high above its floor, making it difficult to walk up. A person must stoop quite low and also watch his footstep that he does not slip. This, according to C. T.

Russell's interpretation, represents the Mosaic Law Dispensation which governed the Israel family from the time the Law was given, up to the time when Christ came and set it aside and started the Christian age of Repentance, Faith and Grace. If this is the case, then for convenience we will call that 1542-inch hall the "Mosaic Hall." During that 1,542 years they had a hard time of it trying to climb up the godly path. It hampered them down and their feet would slip and they grew weary under it; but when Christ came and set before them the new order of things by Repentance, Faith and Grace, *then* they could straighten up and walk unhampered, as represented by the sudden rising of the ceiling to twenty-eight feet high. It will be noticed that the ceiling of the "Mosaic Hall" is only four feet high, while the ceiling of the "Christian Hall" is twenty-eight feet high—just *seven* times the height of the "Mosaic Hall." Seven is a peculiar number; it is odd and yet it balances when placed in a straight line or in a circle. Lay down seven silver dollars in a straight line; one will act as center and have three on each side of it. Leave the center one lie and place the other six around it, so that each of the six will touch *it* and also touch each other; then draw a pencil mark around *all* of them while so arranged together and you will have a perfect circle, with the center of the center dollar as the exact center of the circle; and this circle would balance on a needle-point if it were placed in the central spot. No other number will form a circle and at the same time fill up the center. A *circle* is a complete thing; it has neither beginning nor end; it is *perfection* and goes on and on forever. *Seven* is the law of construction. We read about seven in many places in the Bible.

Some one has looked at this point and writes it out as follows:

"John to the seven churches. Seven candlesticks. The mystery of the seven stars. The Seven Spirits of God. On the seventh day God ended His work. On the seventh month Noah's ark touched the ground. In seven days a dove was sent forth. Abraham pleaded seven times for Sodom. Jacob served seven years for Rachel and seven years more for Leah. Jacob mourned seven days for Joseph. Jacob was pursued seven days' journey by Laban. An abundant season of seven years and a famine of seven years were foretold in Pharaoh's dream by seven fat and seven lean beasts, and seven full and seven thin ears of corn. On the seventh day of the seventh month the children of Israel fasted seven days, and remained seven days in tents. Every seventh year the land rested. Every seventh year all bondmen were set free. Every seventh year the law was read to the people. In the destruction of Jericho, seven priests bore seven trumpets seven days; on the seventh day they surrounded the wall seven times; at the end of the seventh round the wall fell. Solomon was seven years building the Temple and fasted seven days at its dedication. In the Tabernacle were seven lamps, and the golden candlestick had seven branches. Naaman washed seven times in Jordan. Our Savior spoke seven times from the cross, on which He hung seven hours, and after His resurrection appeared on seven different occasions. In the Lord's prayer are seven petitions, containing seven times seven words."—*Ex.*

There is a mystical meaning in numbers, and the ancients used them in connection with their alphabet so that their written words expressed secrets accordingly; and this key is now being discovered, and it is claimed by those who have studied it that the whole Bible is dove-tailed and locked together by numbers which reveal the marvelous wisdom of God in dealing with hidden points.

Christ was the complete one, as represented by the circle which was composed of the seven parts heretofore shown, and, therefore, He has neither beginning nor end.

I am the first and the last. I am alive forever more.—Rev. 1:17, 18.

Therefore, it was a most fitting thing to make the ceiling of the Christian Hall in the Pyramid seven times higher than that of the Mosaic Hall, as the Mosaic Law Dispensation was imperfect and needed only a *four* feet ceiling to represent *it*. You will remember that I have heretofore shown that Prof. Smyth figured back in astronomy and found that in the year 2170 B. C. the seven stars called Pleiades were in exact range with this high-ceiling Christian Hall, so that if the hall could have been extended several million miles into the sky it would have run straight into Pleiades. Pleiades is supposed to be the center of things generally, for this system at least; and our sun and all the planets which we see in the sky circle around Pleiades and draw from it a *good* substance of some kind. The Bible gives us a *hint* that such is the case. The Lord was teaching Job a few lessons to show to him how little Job was; and to press it on Job's mind *thoroughly*, the Lord framed up many questions and put them at the afflicted man, and here is one of them:

Canst thou bind the *sweet* influences of Pleiades?—Job 38:31.

From this we know that the influences from Pleiades are *sweet* (wholesome) and that they are *powerful* so that no *man* can "*bind*" them; therefore, the Mosaic and Christian Halls branched off from the 4044-inch General World Hall and started upward toward Pleiades, so that all who walk in the Mosaic and Christian Hall will eventually arrive at the center of the "*sweet influences.*" As to this center there is a dispute among men. Some say the North Star is the center of all the heavenly planets, and that the sun, moon and stars (except six stars around the North Star) travel around it and that the other six not visible companions of the North Star form the real seven combination which is the center of things. Many times I have watched the movements around the North Star and it *does* seem that every thing goes around it. However this may be, we know that Pleiades gives off sweet influences. It has some uncommon power residing within it. What can it be? The many millions of stars seen in the sky may be *worlds*—some of them being many times larger than this earth, so astronomers tell us. It *may* be that each of these worlds is inhabited by living beings, working out the purposes of God according to their grade of intelligence and spiritual development—each grade occupying a world of its own, with the seven worlds all bundled together, called Pleiades, acting as the "sweet" center for all. All this, mind you, is simply speculation. It would not require much shrewd twisting of Christ's words to make them mean something of this kind, as He says:

In my Father's house are *many* mansions.—John 14:2.

The *whole* universe is God's *house* and these millions of star-worlds *may* be the *mansions* for all we know, as we know nothing about these sayings of Jesus. "Behold, I go to prepare a *place* for thee."

Suppose that God makes His *central* abode in the seven bundled Pleiades (*perfected* place)? It would be easy to understand then why the "*sweet influences*" flow out from Pleiades, and that Job or any other man could not check or "*bind*" them. It would also be easy to understand why the *slant* of the Christian Hall in the stone Pyramid leads straight into Pleiades. In mentioning these things I am not forgetting the fact that "Christ *in you* is the hope of glory" and that it is not "Lo over here or lo over there, but that the kingdom of God is *within you.*" Yes, the spiritual Christ must be in each person and then that person is in the kingdom of God, whether he be on this earth or elsewhere. The kingdom of God is wherever the man is with Christ in him; but the Father's house with its many mansions are worthy of thought, even though it may not refer to locations.

At the point where the Mosaic Hall branches off from the General World Hall a large stone plug, 179 inches long is tightly fitted into the Mosaic Hall so that the only way to gain entrance to the Mosaic Hall is by a passage-way cut through the rock at the *side* of the plug so that one can walk around the obstruction (plug) and start up the Mosaic Hall. Mr. Russell, who has carefully studied the matter, claims that God intended that the 179-inch plug length should be added onto the length of the hall to make it express the correct number of years that elapsed from the time the Twelve Tribes of Israel left Egypt to the year 36 A. D. He claims that the plug should be drawn out its full length, like drawing out a telescope before taking the measure of the hall, and that the plug should be counted as hall. You will naturally wonder why God did not make the Pyramid a little larger so that the hall could be its full length without the plug. This may be easily answered when you know that the foundation or base of the Pyramid had to be just so many feet square to express the exact length of time in four years, and also to make the diagonal measurements express the number of years (25,827) in the precessional period—the length of time required for the sun to make a circle around Pleiades. At the end of the Mosaic Hall and on a level with it and going upward at the same angle, sets in the Christian Hall (I name it this for convenience). It is simply an extension of the Mosaic Hall, only the Christian Hall ceiling is twenty-eight feet high; and the length of the hall (measured on the floor line) is represented by three sets of figures as follows: 1874 inches from north end to a stone step at south end; then omitting the rise of the step by raising the measuring line to the top edge of step and going on to end of hall.

The next measurement is 1881 inches by going *through* the step as though it were not there.

The next is 1910 inches by commencing at north end of hall and going to the step—then measuring upward to top of step; then back to south end of hall.

That stone step was put there for a purpose, evidently, and the measurements to it, over it and *through* it certainly have a meaning; and some have ventured an interpretation, but I shall pass the matter without comment. It is enough to know that we have arrived almost to the point where the four winds will be let loose as described in Rev. 7:1, 2,

3, and that the most dreadful and scorching tribulation that ever struck this earth will then be upon a grasping, proud and foolish people; and it will probably mow down two-thirds of the inhabitants of the world, while the remaining third will be brought through the fires of purification and made pure.

And it shall come to pass that in all the land, two parts therein shall be cut off and die, but the third shall be left. And I will bring the third part through the fire and will refine them as silver is refined, and will try them as gold is tried. They shall call on my name and I will hear them. I will say, It is my people; and they shall say, The Lord is our God.—Zech. 13:8, 9.

The choosing and sifting of the Elect Body of persons are now going on and the Lord is testing them and putting them through what He is pleased to call the refiner's fire.

He is like a refiner's fire. He shall sit as a refiner and purifier.—Mal. 3:2, 3.

All this training seems to be marked in the stone Pyramid in a peculiar way. The stone step, heretofore mentioned, is located near the end of the Christian Hall. The traveler comes to the step which is three feet high, and after climbing up to its top surface he finds himself on a level floor, not slanting; a few feet further is the end of the hall with a very low door-way through which the pilgrim passes into a little room called the Ante-Chamber with a granite floor. The floor all the way up through the Mosaic and Christian Halls is of limestone, but the pilgrim having stood the testing and self-sacrifice and kept the straight path, the Lord now gives him a granite (fine) floor and makes it horizontal without any slant upward; but before he could reach this foundation for his feet he had to bow down very low through the

Refiner's fire to pass through the low door leading from the Christian Hall to the Ante-Chamber; here he finds himself with plenty of room and probably remains a short time to receive further teaching from God. Each of the four walls of this Chamber has peculiarities belonging to itself and not found in any of the other walls. In some, grooves are cut. God has not yet let men into the mysteries carved in them. We are just now about to pass out of the Christian Hall. We have gone through the fires of affliction, trouble and distraction, in order to sweep from us our old ways, but we are not yet through. We must make further sacrifices. A few more years yet and that Ante-Chamber will be understood. Having received its lessons, the pilgrim passes on and comes to another low door leading *out* of it. He bows down while passing a short distance through it and suddenly finds himself in an elegant room, a brief description of which Mr. Henry F. Gordon writes as follows:

"It is a very noble apartment 34 feet long, 17 feet broad and 19 feet high; of polished *red granite* throughout; walls, floor and ceiling in blocks squared true and joined together with such exquisite skill that no autocrat emperor of modern times could desire anything more solidly noble and refined. The only thing this chamber contains is an empty (granite) coffer (stone box) without a lid; and it is worthy of notice that this coffer corresponds with the sacred Ark of the Mosaic Tabernacle in capacity."

Thus we see that the pilgrim of God, after climbing up the steep slanted Mosaic and the Christian Halls and stooping very low to pass through the low doors leading into the Ante-Chamber and from there into this great King's Chamber, finds himself surrounded by polished surfaces on all sides—below, above and at the sides. He has landed, at last, in the King's Chamber sure enough. He is dwelling in the same room with God, as the granite box sitting there indicates. When the Twelve Tribes of Israel were on their forty years journey from Egypt to Palestine they carried with them the Ark of the Covenant, which was a box covered inside and outside with gold. The Lord claimed that He would be in the box which was kept in a room made for it. No one but Aaron, the High Priest, was allowed to go into that room. If any other persons touched the box it would kill them. Some ventured to it, but they fell over dead. It was to represent the Lord and His dwelling place; and the stone box in the King's Chamber tells the weary pilgrim that he has at last arrived at the head-quarters of God. This great King's Chamber and also the Ante-room are in the center of the Pyramid. Ventilating passages lead from the outside into these rooms.

Having traced the halls from the outside entrance of the Pyramid up to the final end called the King's Chamber, let us now go back to an important spot which I purposely omitted in tracing them upward, as I was calling attention to *lengths* principally, in order to show dates and times when *this* dispensation or Age would close and when the Millennial Age will set in, as that seems to be the absorbing question with the people, although in *reality*, the *main* point is the gaining of the high spiritual condition (on this earth) that will lead us up into the King's Chamber and dwell with God (here, on earth). It is that high spiritual goodness pointed out by the Lord's Prayer:

Thy kingdom come when Thy will be done *in earth* as it is done in heaven.—*Lord's Prayer.*

You must not forget that the kingdom of God is *within* you and that your body is earthy and that when the Spirit is working through you and commanding you then the King (Christ) is in earth and you are doing the will or going according to the directions of the Spirit, and then His will is being done *in earth* as in heaven. This is the kingdom of God *in earth*. This is why Christ told the apostles to say unto the people that the kingdom of God had come nigh unto them. The Spirit (God) working through the apostles, and they following Its or His dictates was the kingdom of God, as the King had full control, and as an apostle would come near a person that person was near the workings of the kingdom of God. This particular point about the kingdom of God, as to *where* it is and *what* it is, can not be mentioned too often, as the general belief of the people on this subject is *all* wrong; and it has done untold damage to the world in *many* ways. The people *imagine* that the kingdom of God is located away off, and that a person must die before he can go to it; and when we tell them that men should be so closely in union with God as to hear His voice and be directed by Him and talk with Him they think it is the rankest kind of insanity; and they are *quick* to say that "the day of miracles is past," and that God *could not* and *will not* speak to any person on earth nowadays. They give the "lie" to Christ's words at once when He says:

The kingdom of God is *within* you.—Luke 17:21. God's will be done *in earth* (not in the sky) as it is done in heaven. —*Lord's Prayer.* Ye are the temple of God.—2 Cor. 6:16. Your body is the temple of the Holy Ghost which is in you. —1 Cor. 6:19.

It was this mystery, about the close relation of man to God, which Christ came to teach. God (Christ) took on flesh and walked around among men and ate and talked with them to show to them who and what they were, and that it is possible for flesh-men to be in union with and under the direct guidance of the Supreme King.

He that believeth on me, the works that I do shall he do also, and *greater* works than these shall he do.—John 14:12.

The time for the revealing of this mystery of God in man is marked in the halls of the Pyramid. The Twelve Tribes of Israel had journeyed up the long period of over 1,500 years, as represented by the Mosaic Hall; and suddenly the ceiling rose to twenty-eight feet; here the Christ (God in the flesh) stepped on earth to reveal to men the Mystery about God dwelling in man.

Even the mystery which hath been hid from ages and generations, but now is made manifest to his saints: which is Christ (God) in you, the hope of glory—Colossians 1:26, 27.

There (where the high ceiling commenced) the God-man (Jesus) was born. He dwelt among men until He was thirty-three years old, when His *fleshly* career ended; this is marked in the stone floor by a hole or rough aperture located just thirty-three inches from the point where the Christian Hall (high ceiling) begins. It has the appearance of having been blasted out, as it is irregular and torn, as though the explosion had been powerful. Mr. Russell holds that the exploded appearance was made there by the builders to represent the resurrection of Christ. Nothing could hold Him. Death had no power over Him. The bounds of the tomb broke away and He came forth with victory.

All power in heaven and in earth is given unto me.—Matt. 28:18.

This explosion point is called, by writers of to-day, the *"well."* From it leads, almost straight down, another passage through the rock and passes far below the foundation of the Pyramid and meets the General World, 4044 inch, hall. The New Testament (Matt. 12:40) tells us that as Jonah was three days and nights in the belly of the fish so was Christ three days and nights in the heart of the earth. It is also stated that while the fleshly body of Jesus was lying in the tomb those three days His spirit or real self was away, preaching to the spirits of persons who were in prison ever since the Flood. (See 1 Peter 3:19, 20.) No doubt they were persons who refused to heed Noah's warnings, and, of course, the Flood came and swept them to death; and as they had never paid any attention to spiritual things they were ignorant of God's spiritual laws and, of course, had no knowledge of their way out of their terrible predicament. They were in prison sure enough. They had wasted their time on this earth in just such foolishness as people are now doing and when the disaster took them they had no Helper, and Christ left His body lie there in the tomb while He *descended* to where these prisoners were and preached to them. This passage leading down from the "exploded" aperture (the "well") *may* represent His journey to the prisoners, as they were, evidently, on a lower plane of existence than He was and He would be represented as going *down* to them; and the fact that this downward passage runs into the descending General World Hall shows that He had to go to the same level of life as those prisoners had occupied before the Flood took them. This theory about this downward hall is purely speculation. While speaking of these prisoners it seems proper to call attention to the fact that God did not put them in prison; *they put themselves* there by their own foolishness. While they were in the flesh, on earth, they sought nothing but gratification on the material line, such as good things to eat, fine, showy things to wear and sexual associations to their heart's content and a general wasted life, such as the people *now* are living; and when the flesh bodies were taken from them by death they had no education in the spiritual line, and their likes and dislikes were not in harmony with the spiritual company over there, and there was no attraction to draw them together into the company of Love. There was a wide gulf between the two classes and those on the lower or beastly plane had no "magnet" to draw them across that "gulf." They were actually imprisoned, with no attractions to help them out of their low plane. They had been there ever since the Flood, and Christ went to teach them. While they were on earth they would not hear teaching on spiritual subjects. Noah tried 120 years to reach them with a bit of knowledge, but they turned their backs to him and said, "That old 'krank' is always harping about spiritual things and such 'stuff.' He is a regular nuisance in the neighborhood. We care nothing for his 'gab.' We are going to have a good (?) time."

The ideas the people have about a "good time" are a *delusion*. It is *actual insanity*. The criminal who delights in robbing trains, killing people, becoming intoxicated and rolling in the mud is looked upon as being deluded and not knowing what a "good time" is. He looks at it through wrong eyes and with a wrong mind, therefore, he is insane; but those who condemn him are doing the same thing, only on a little different plane. They are running after things just as worthless and as destructive, and yet they say they are having a "good time." Insanity again. The criminal violates the law and the law hangs him. Just so it is on the spiritual line. A person violates and runs across the spiritual laws and they cut him in pieces, and he has no power to climb out because he is ignorant of spiritual things. The person who refuses to go to school and learn arithmetic knows nothing of its rules by which problems can be solved. He is left to the mercy of others to help him out of his troubles. He is in prison when he falls into business troubles requiring arithmetic to help him out. He can not handle it; neither can *it* handle *him*, as it can not come in touch with his mind. God did not put him in such a predicament; he put himself there by refusing to learn the mysterious rules which would lift him out. At the time when he *should* have learned them his mind was deluded into the idea of having a "good time," never realizing the day of trouble just ahead that would require a knowledge of arithmetic. The world to-day is in the same delusion—grabbing after dollars and piling up great heaps of property and living for the stomach and fleshly gratifications—never realizing the day of trouble just ahead that will require a *perfect* knowledge of the spiritual laws of faith in God to shield them from the plagues and *terrible* tribulations which will sweep over the earth between 1896 to 1915, after which there will be more "prisoners," made such by their own acts—just as it was in the days of Noah. The Pyramid seems to show all this, but before passing to that point another hall comes in for its share of teaching. It starts at the "well" (exploded aperture) and runs horizontally to the center of the Pyramid, where it terminates in a room called the Queen's Chamber. I shall venture no interpretation on this hall and its room. It has a purpose, whatever that purpose may be, as it was not put there by chance.

We now come to the General World Hall, which, as heretofore mentioned, is 4044 inches long. The human family has been coming down that hall ever since 2170 B. C. You will remember that Prof. Smyth, the astronomer, figured it back and found that the slant of the hall pointed towards the Dragon star at that date; if the hall could have been extended millions of miles into the sky it would have run straight into the Dragon. The Scriptures always refer to *dragon* as evil.

And I saw an angel come down from heaven, having the key of the bottomless pit, and a great chain in his hand; and he laid hold on the *dragon*, that old serpent, which is the devil, and Satan, and bound him a thousand years, and cast him into the bottomless pit.—Rev. 20:1-3.

Thus we see that this General World Hall was in line with the evil *named* star, and that the people would travel down that line towards the "pit," which is at the end of the hall and 100 feet below the foundation of the Pyramid. The "pit" is a room 46x28 feet cut in the natural rock of the earth. All the other rooms heretofore mentioned are in the Pyramid proper and were built there as the stone were laid by the workmen; but this "pit" is down in the natural rock 100 feet below the base line of the Pyramid—showing that the human family would not stop at the *floor* line of God's solid house, but would go on lower into the earth. "Earth" and "earthy" are always mentioned as the *opposite* of spiritual things; and indeed history and general observation at this time show this to be the case. The people like the "earthy" things—things of this earth. The *heavenly* things—things of the Spirit are not attractive to the general public. There is no *"fun"* in it they say. No gratification of the fleshly wants and lusts and appetites. They prefer the "earthy." They want to go on *down* in the earth. Every thing that is foolish, absurd and *destructive* is sought after, now, with *intense* delight. If any of the grand and powerful things of the Spirit are mentioned the company will scatter as though small-pox had been thrown among them. Some will have important household duties to look after immediately; others will see some *very* "funny" thing occurring out doors, while another will be anxious to know how the marriage turned out in the love-story. I mention these things to show that the world is going in *precisely* the same way that it did in Noah's time. They *would not* hear or heed. They rushed on to the mad dance of death and found themselves in "prison" afterwards while Noah and his family escaped the disaster by relying on God. *They* were the *Elect* family at *that* turn of the dispensations; whereas the Elect Body of people, who are to escape the plagues and disaster soon to set in, are just now being brought together and trained for the terrible ordeal. They are those who give up everything and turn themselves over to do His will regardless of the scoffing of the world. Lot did this and hurried out of the cities of Sodom and Gomorrah, and the earth opened and, with fiery blasts, swallowed those cities as though they were gnats; and their locations are marked to this day by salt-encrusted and sulphur lumps lying around their sites.

The people of Pompeii and Herculaneum were living a riotous life and seeking the "earthy" things and they *got* them, but not as they wished. It was more "earthy" than was pleasant. The great fiery volcano bursted out and spewed the bowels of the earth up into the air to fall down in a red-hot melted condition and cover up and bury those cities. The workmen who are now digging down to the ancient foundations find loaves of bread in the ovens. They were baking when the disaster struck the cities in the year 74 A. D. The people then were at their daily work—never even dreaming of the *terrible* upheaval that was going on in the earth to burst out and cover them.

While these two cities have no bearing on the Pyramid subject now being treated, except to show the desperate and downward course of the people into ungodliness and the fearful end to which they come, as marked by the slant of the General World Hall with its "pit" at the lower end, 100 feet below the surface of earth, I think I will be excused and justified for digressing from the main subject a moment to set out a brief history of the terrible calamity which struck these cities, so that your mind can better realize what the prophecies are talking about when they say that the Lord will come forth out of His holy habitation to shake terribly the earth—Isa. 2:12, 19; and that those who are proud and haughty will be brought *low;* and the unearthing of those two cities (Pompeii and Herculaneum) shows the miserable condition into which the people were plunged unaware. The description of the findings now being uncovered is written by Mr. H. B. Brumbaugh, of Pennsylvania, U. S., who visited the ruins a few months ago and writes from there under date of Sept. 24, 1895, and the *Gospel Messenger* publishes the letter as follows:

We are now at Naples, known the world over for her volcano and buried cities Pompeii and Herculaneum. The buried cities, however, are sights of no ordinary character, and no one should miss seeing Pompeii when passing through Naples. The founding of the city dates away back some four or five hundred years before Christ. About the year 72 A. D. it was partly destroyed by an earthquake, but was rebuilt, and two years afterwards it was covered over or buried in ashes from an eruption of Vesuvius, some twenty feet deep, when over twenty thousand of the inhabitants were destroyed. For centuries the dead slept in their unknown tombs, but gradually discoveries of the buried city were made. Excavations were made, but not to any considerable extent until A. D. 1872. Since then, the work has been pushed forward more rapidly until the greater part of the city is now uncovered. As we entered this resurrected city, we experienced feelings that were peculiar and sad. We imagined a city of fifty thousand or more, all astir at their callings. The chariots, with spirited horses in silver-embellished harness, seemed rushing through the streets; the merchants busy selling their wares; the shopmen attending to their trade; the barber plying the razor and the scissors; the soap manufacturer busy preparing his material; the baker just put his bread in the oven; the lady of leisure at her toilet, and the promenaders, in full dress, on the street. All at once the thunderings of Vesuvius are heard, the heavens are darkened, and the hot ashes, in stifling thickness, descend upon the now terror-stricken inhabitants. In a few moments the King of Terrors waved over the fated city his sword of power, and all was quite. A deep sleep had fallen upon the inhabitants, and the living, active, pleasure-loving city of a few moments before is now the dead and buried city of Pompeii. Such seems to have been the ending of this city, as we would infer from the evidences found in the excavations made. In the museum are seen casts of the bodies of men and beasts, just as they were when death so suddenly met them. As they were thus buried, the moisture from the bodies dampened the ashes by which they were surrounded. As it then dried, it hardened, thus forming a perfect mould of the body it encased. Through time, the bodies mouldered into dust, and the moulds that surrounded them were left almost empty. When the excavations were made, these moulds of dead bodies were found, and the thought of getting casts of them was at once suggested. When one was found, the presence of which was plainly indicated by the hollow sound as heard by the excavator, it was approached carefully and an opening made into the mould. The little dust left in it was removed and the mould poured full of plaster of Paris, which soon hardened, and a complete reproduction of the decayed bodies was had. To see these, and carefully examine the different positions in which death found them, is an interesting study. Some of the bodies were lying face upward, some on their side, and others face downward. In some of the faces are seen the expression of the agonies of death; while in others, the peacefulness of sleep.

Among the casts to which we gave special notice, was that of a medium-sized dog, lying on his back,—legs pushed upward and drawn together, with neck stretched out and head turned or twisted downward, depicting the most painful agonies of death.

Looking at the costly and richly embellished halls, palaces, theatres, and residences, with the extensive provisions made for pleasure and enjoyment, in connection with the suddenness in which death came to the inhabitants, and we cannot help being impressed with the terrible scene, as it looms up before us, and we were made to think of what Paul says: "For when they shall say, Peace and safety, then sudden destruction cometh upon them, as travail upon a woman with child; and they shall not escape."—*Brumbaugh's letter in Messenger.*

Just so it is with the people of to-day. They talk arbitration and hold peace conferences when there is no peace and cannot be, with the people in their present rebellious attitude against God and His New Age, which He is pressing onto the earth rapidly and the people are up in arms against Him and the commotion is terrible all over the world. Society is falling to pieces; governments are trembling and wabbling like a ship in a storm, trying to keep above the dashing waves. Churches, *long* ago, run off the track and "took to the woods" and are marauding around with the remainder of the world, without any spirituality or even sound *morality*. They know not God. Organizations of every conceivable kind are being formed and will be "in line" to perform their part in the mad dance. And while things on earth are being shaped for the fell sweep the elements of the atmosphere are changing, so that frosts steal in on us during the hot days of summer, and floods and drouths walk hand in hand, with scarcely a line between them, so that one farm will burn up for want of moisture while the one joining it will drown to death. The whole heavens are rumbling with trouble that will shake to pieces the kingdoms of this world and sweep them into the "pit"—never again to rise, as the dark room under the Pyramid clearly indicates. Starting in at the upper end of the hall, at the finely ruled line near the door, on north side of the Pyramid, they came downward 628 years (inches); then Abraham, Father of the Twelve Tribes of Israel, withdrew from the other nations and turned off and upward into another hall, which, for convenience, I have named *Mosaic* Hall. He and his descendants through Jacob went upward through that hall, learning the ways of God, 1,500 years or more, while the general world kept straight on downward 3,092 years (inches) further until the hall suddenly ceases to slant by running horizontally (on a level) 324 inches (years), and then comes the "pit" (dark room cut in natural rock).

The point where the hall ceased slanting downward is 1,550 inches (years) past the birth of Christ; hence it should read 1550 A. D. Here something took place that put a stop to the downward course of the people, spiritually. They did not run *upward* into light, but they simply kept on a level—not falling into any further darkness. They *had* been, during the previous 1,400 years, falling into darkness more and more, but now, at this point, they ceased to go lower. None but the close students of history have any knowledge of the terrible and dreadful darkness of the people from about 300 years after Christ's ascension to 1800 A. D. It was too terrible to describe. All writers *now* refer to that period as the *Dark Age*. The teachings of Christ had been almost exterminated, root and branch; there was just a mere speck left and *that* even had to be kept covered and hidden away from the great beast that roamed over the earth 1,260 years, devouring every thing. The history of that thing almost stops a person's heart from beating and takes the breath. Its career was one of general terror, confiscation and murder. Its path, from beginning to end, was strewn with blood and tears. It is beyond the power of the human mind to understand why God permitted such a *terrible* hyena to spring out upon the people and devour them and destroy the seeds of goodness which Christ had sown. But I am not finding fault with God, mind you, as His way is perfect, but our human understanding does not grasp His reasons for *permitting* certain things which we, as human beings, would dash to pieces instantly; but God is both patient and merciful. He fully understood, of *course*, that such a thing as this hyena *would* be, as He inspired His prophets, hundreds of years before, and also His apostles, to write its history hundreds of years before the *beast* appeared. It came walking in on time, as set by them, and it commenced its bloody career by drawing its razor across the throat of the world and sitting down on it and holding possession the dreadfully long period of 1,260 years. It was like an eclipse on the sun during all that time. It shut off the light and the people fell into the blackness of night and stampeded and devoured each other in the most horrifying manner. All the books now in the world could not contain a complete history of the devastating deeds and horrors produced by this beast. It was a monster. God's prophets, who were on earth many hundred years before the beast came, wrote out a brief description of what it would be, as follows:

> I saw in the vision a fourth beast, dreadful and terrible and strong exceedingly. It had great iron teeth and devoured and brake in pieces and stamped the residue. It had ten horns. There came up among the ten horns another little horn; it had eyes like the eyes of man and a mouth speaking great things; and it made war with the saints (Christ's followers) and it prevailed against them.
>
> He shall speak great words against the Most High and change times and laws and wear out the Saints of the Most High and they shall be given over into his (the beast's) hand until a time and times and the dividing of time (1260 years). —Daniel 7.

The little horn that sprang up and became a monster is the beast to which I draw attention especially, as it grew and spread over the world and spoke great things; and you will notice that the prophet said that it would make war with the saints and overcome them and *wear* them out and change times and laws to suit its own purposes.

> It cast down the Truth to the ground and it (the beast) practiced and prospered and magnified itself even greater than the Prince (Christ) and it (the beast) waxed great.—Daniel 8.

The beast finally proclaimed itself greater than Christ and cast His teachings down to the ground and prospered greatly. Much more is said in the prophecies about this great beast, but I pass on to a time several hundred years later and note what the apostles saw concerning this beast that would arise after they (the apostles) would leave the earth.

Saint John the revelator in his vision describes it as follows:

I saw a beast rise up having seven heads and ten horns and upon his heads the name of BLASPHEMY. And the *dragon* (devil) gave the beast *his* power and *his* seat and *great* authority; and *all the world* wondered after the beast; and they worshiped the dragon (devil) which gave power unto the beast; and they worshiped the beast, and said, Who is like the beast? Who is able to war with him? And there was given to the beast a mouth speaking great things and blasphemies. And he opened his mouth in blasphemy *against* God to blaspheme His name and His tabernacle. And it was given unto the beast to make war with the saints and *overcome them.* And power was given the beast over *all* nations.—Rev. 13.

Notice that the Scripture positively points out that the beast was a tool or agent of the dragon (devil) and that the dragon gave up his own seat to the beast and turned over his power to the beast and that it (the beast) ruled over all nations, and became so great that people declared that nothing could war with it. It had every body completely under it, so that if any thing came up against the beast the whole world had to come to its help and slay the opposition. The beast boycotted and murdered every body who refused to stand up for it. If a merchant or any kind of a business man was a little weak about standing up for the beast, orders went out to boycott him, so that no one dare buy any thing from him or sell to him unless he would come into the ranks and agree with the beast.

And he (the beast) caused all, both small and great, rich and poor, free and slave, to receive a mark (the cross) in their right hand or in their forehead, so that no man might buy or sell unless he had the mark or the name of the beast or the number of his name, for his number is the number of a man; and his number is 666.—Rev. 13.

Now you will say that if we could only understand the above description of the beast and his number (666) we could find him on the earth somewhere and could then see who he is and what he looks like. Well, by a queer circumstance, I am pleased to be able to lay before you some part of the mystery and exhibit a photograph of the man himself, as the above scripture tells us that it is a *man*, and that his *number* is 666. This chapter was written, and this beast was thoroughly discussed and shown and the manuscript laid away, ready for the printer, when, suddenly and unexpectedly, a California paper came floating along through the mail to me, and, on examining its columns, I found an article discussing this identical beast and figuring out his number (666) and showing a picture of its head man, the pope. The article had been copied from *The American*, published at San Diego, California, from which (by permission) I copy it in full although it is not *entirely* correct as I view it, as the scriptures seem to say there is a beast and an image and a number, etc. But this article brings forth a clew which leads to a starting point, from which the mystery may be unraveled. It is proper to state here that in ancient time the letters of their alphabet had a certain value in figures. That is, each letter represented a certain number, so that when certain letters were put together to spell a name, the number of that name would depend on what letters were used in it.

666.

THE NUMBER OF THE BEAST IS THAT OF A MAN.

Editor of The American:

The Bible, with its wonderful store of information, is every day being more thoroughly understood and appreciated by the thoughtful students of God's Word; and passages which even a few years ago men's minds were unable fully to comprehend, are now easily unravelled, and their true meaning clearly conveyed to the inquiring mind searching for the truth. Rome, therefore, will not, nor never did, allow her followers to read the Word of God, fearing they might become enlightened and she would rather bring them up in total ignorance than permit them to read the gospel.

Now let us refer to Rev. 13:18 and see what it means. The words are: "Here is wisdom. Let him that hath understanding count the number of the beast; for it is the number of a man, and his number is 666." This appears at

A ROMAN CATHOLIC POPE.

first sight to be a difficult verse to decipher; and while the Romish priests have asserted that it referred to the Mohammedan church, Protestant theologians have thought differently, but now we can produce proof positive that it refers to the pope of Rome and his church. You ask for the proof; well, you shall have it.

Take a look at the engraving of a pope with his pontifical mitre or crown and the inscription upon it in letters of gold, just as he wears it and as his predecessors have worn it for centuries in the dark past. Notice the words upon the pope's mitre: "Vicarius Filii Dei," the English of which is "A SUBSTITUTE FOR THE SON OF GOD." Now this Latin inscription in Latin letters has another signification, which at first sight is likely to be overlooked. For instance, many Latin letters were used as numerals as well as letters. To illustrate this fact just take out your watch and you will find on its face the Latin letter "I" for one, two "II's" stand for 2. "V" or "U" are used indiscriminately and either one stands for 5. "X" stands for 10. All the hour marks on your watch or clock are Roman or Latin letters which also denote the number of the hour, yet there are many letters in the Latin alphabet which have no significance at all as numerals.

The quotation from Revelation says "the number of the beast which is the number of a man is 666." Now let us see if the Word of God does not point out to us the beast and clearly prove the pope of Rome to be the 666, from the very words inscribed on his crown, "Vicarius Filii Dei." the Roman numerals reading as follows:

V	means	5	F	means	0	D	means	500
I	"	1	I	"	1	E	"	0
C	"	100	L	"	50	I	"	1
A	"	0	I	"	1			———
R	"	0	I	"	1			501
I	"	1						
U	"	5			53			
S	"	0						

———
112

The numerals in **Vicarius** are 112
The numerals in **Filii** are   53
The numerals in **Dei** are   501
———
666

The letters A R F S E and many others of the Latin alphabet do not represent any number and never did.

By adding these together we find the number 666, the exact number which God has declared to be the "number of the beast which is the number of a man," making it conclusively evident that the pope and the papacy are the beast referred to. Such being the case, is it not astonishing how little our ministers of the gospel have to say upon the subject? Why do not they preach openly against this great arch-enemy of Christianity, of progress, and of civilization? Can it be because they fear to suffer, as Peter feared when he denied our Lord? If so, let them act with more courage in the future, as Peter did.

There are some Pauls among us still who dare to preach,

openly and boldly, without fear or favor, the whole truth of God's Word. How much better for the world would it be if there were more of them.   Chaplain.

Having shown his number and photograph, let us look for his mark, which prophecy says he will have. I quote from the same paper (*The American*) on this point.

THE MARK.

THE SIGN OF THE CROSS MADE WITH ASHES.

Placed on All Good Catholics on Ash Wednesday—More of the Roman Beast.

Editor American:

That the pope and the Roman hierarchy represent the beast referred to in the last verse of the 13th chapter of Revelation, has been proven; let us show another of the many existing proofs to the same effect.

Read Rev. 13:16 and you will find these words in reference to the popish power (the beast): "And he causeth all, both small and great, rich and poor, free and bond, to receive the mark in their right hand or in their foreheads." Let us see how this applies to the Roman hierarchy. What is this mark in their right hands or in their foreheads which the followers of the beast are said to receive? Well, it is simply as scripture states, "a mark" which is made by the priests of Rome upon the foreheads of all the followers of the pope, "small and great, rich and poor," every Ash Wednesday, which isthe first day of Lent, and is called by the priests *caput jejunii.*

Now let us quote from the American Encyclopedia, Vol. II. Under the heading "Ash Wednesday" it says: "In the Roman Catholic Church on this day the priest makes the sign of the cross with ashes on the foreheads of the people, repeating the words, *Memento homo quod pulvis es, et in pulverem reverteris.*" This is the mark of the beast and is practiced over the whole world where Roman Catholics are to be found.

In Ireland, Italy, French Canada, Mexico, Newfoundland and other countries, where the masses of the people are Catholics and intensely ignorant, this "mark upon their foreheads" is daubed on so as to be seen many yards distant upon the public streets and none would think of removing it for fear of committing what they call a mortal sin. Nature and time alone are allowed to efface it, soap and water never. But here in enlightened America, where education and Protestantism prevail, these "holy ashes," as they call them, are laid on with a lighter hand by the Romish clergy. The writer knows of a case where a refined young Catholic lady, a native daughter, had to devote several dollars to a saint before she could induce the "holy father" to make the smutmark on her forehead as light as possible. This smutmark is "the mark of the beast," and that beast is the papacy. Chaplain.

Let us now examine another peculiar feature which the beast was to have. He was to have a peculiar or unusual mouth which would speak great things and blaspheme against God by appropriating to himself (the beast) the things belonging to God; that is, the beast would call himself God and the Most High and the Supreme Ruler and Holy Father and other great names and powers which belong to none other than God.

And there was given unto him (the beast) a mouth, speaking great things. And he shall speak great words against the Most High and blaspheme God's name.—Rev. 13:5, 6. Daniel 7:8-25.

Now turn to all of the histories and other books of church, written by Roman Catholics, and your hair will almost stand up and bristle as you read the high swelling titles and names which they give to the pope of Rome. They call him *"Christ by Unction"; "Holy Father"; "Physician of Souls"; "Apostolic Lord"; "Prince of the Universe"; "Priest and King"; "Head of All the Holy Priests of God"; "Key-Bearer of the Kingdom of Heaven"* and many other high names which apply to none but God, yet this beast takes them unto himself. And the high officers of the Catholic church, when writing of the pope, declare that the pope has *"power to shut heaven and send the guilty to hell"*; and that *"he can judge all persons, but can not be judged by any"*; and that *"he is only a little lower than an angel."*

"He is crowned so that the faithful may kiss his feet." "Thou art he to whom the keys of heaven are given." "Canst thou not shut up heaven?" "The pope is of such dignity and highness that he is not simply a man, but God, and is crowned as king of heaven, of earth and of hell."

If the Catholic writers who wrote all of the above high-sounding titles would have stopped at the last one, which says "the pope is king of hell," they would have been in better line, as the Bible tells us that the devil got up out of his seat and told the pope ("beast") to sit down in it and commence to rule in the devil's place.

And I saw a beast of seven heads (seven hills of Rome); and the dragon gave him his seat and his power and great authority.—Rev. 13:1, 2.

As further evidence that the Roman Catholic church with its popes is the great beast having a blasphemous mouth speaking great swelling words and blasphemy against the Most High, just as St. John's book of Revelation declares it would, I now introduce some of the popes' writings from time to time, declaring themselves *God, Christ, All in All and Above All* and many other terrible and astounding blasphemies. They almost make one's heart flutter while reading them. Now hear their printed utterances copied from histories and other books and set forth by the English author H. G. Guinness. Think as you read and you will see how true St. John's visions were.

A ROMAN CATHOLIC POPE'S DECREE.

Wherefore, seeing such power is given to Peter, and to me in Peter, being his successor, who is he then in all the world that ought not to be subject to my decree, which have such power in heaven, in hell, in earth, with the quick and also the dead? By the jurisdiction of which key the fullness of my power is so great that, whereas all others are subjects —yea, and emperors themselves ought to subdue their executions to me—only I am subject to no creature, no, not to myself; so my Papal majesty ever remaineth undiminished; superior to all men, whom all persons ought to obey and follow, whom no man must judge or accuse of any crime, no man depose but I myself. No man can excommunicate me, yea, though I commune with the excommunicated; for no man bindeth me: whom no man must lie to, for he that lieth to me is a heretic, and an excommunicated person. Thus, then, it appeareth that the greatness of priesthood began in Melchisedec, was solemnized in Aaron, perfectionated in Christ, represented in Peter, exalted in the universal jurisdiction and manifested in the Pope. So that through this pre-eminence of my priesthood having all things subject to me, it may seem well verified in me, that was spoken of Christ, Thou hast subdued all things under his feet.

And likewise, it is to be presumed that the bishop of that church is always good and holy. Yea, though he fall into homicide or adultery, he may sin, but yet he cannot be accused, but rather excused by the murders of Samson, the thefts of the Hebrews, etc. All the earth is my diocese, and I have the authority of the King of all kings upon subjects. I am all in all, and above all, so that God himself, and I, the vicar of God, have both one consistory, and I am able to do almost all that God can do. In all things that I list my will is to stand for reason, for I am able by the law to dispense above the law, and of wrong to make justice in correcting laws and changing them. Wherefore, if those things that I do be said not to be done of man, but of God— What can you make me but God? Again, if prelates of the church be called and counted of Constantine for God, I then, being above all prelates, seem by this reason to be above all Gods. Wherefore, no marvel if it be in my power to change time, to alter and abrogate laws, to dispense with all things, yea, with the precepts of Christ: (*Yes, the Roman Church sets aside Christ's teaching*) for where Christ biddeth Peter put up his sword, and admonishes His disciples not to use any outward force in revenging themselves, do not I. Pope Nicholas writing to the bishops of France, exhort them to draw out their material swords? * * * And, whereas Christ was present himself at the marriage in Cana of

Galilee, do not I, Pope Martin, in my distinction, inhibit the spiritual clergy to be present at marriage-feasts, and also to marry? Moreover, where Christ biddeth us lend without hope of gain, do not I, Pope Martin, give dispensation for the same? What should I speak of murder, making it to be no murder or homicide to slay them that be excommunicated? Likewise, against the law of nature, item against the apostles, I can and do dispense; for where they command a priest for fornication to be deposed, I, through the authority of Sylvester, do alter the rigor of that constitution, considering the minds and bodies also of men now to be weaker than they were then. If ye list briefly to hear the whole number of all such cases as properly do appertain to my Papal dispensation, which come to the number of one-and-fifty points, that no man may meddle with but only I myself alone, I will recite them. (Here follows the list.) After that I have now sufficiently declared my power in earth, in heaven, in purgatory, how great it is, and what is the fulness thereof in binding, loosing, commanding, permitting, electing, confirming, dispensing, doing and undoing, etc. I will speak now a little of my riches and of my great possessions, that every man may see my wealth and abundance of all things—rents, tithes, tributes; my silks, my purple mitres, crowns, gold, silver, pearls and gems, lands and lordships.

These are exactly the things which St. John says the seven-headed beast (the Roman church) would have.

Alas, that great city (Rome and the pope) that was clothed in fine linen, purple and scarlet and decked with gold, precious stones and pearls.—Rev. 18:16. And the woman (pope and his church) was arrayed in purple and scarlet color and decked with gold and precious stones and pearls, having a golden cup in her hand, full of abominations.—Rev. 17:4.

The golden cup, mentioned above, is probably the golden cup now used by the Roman Catholic priests at their Mass, when the cup is filled with wine and the priest holds it up in front of a gold image and claims that the wine is transformed into pure blood of Christ. The priest then drinks it for the congregation and they claim that it is a *new* sacrifice each time it is done; whereas, the New Testament tells us that Christ's death was a *continual* sacrifice forever. This is why the Catholic golden cup is full of abominations, because it claims to hold a new lot of *actual* blood and a *new* sacrifice manufactured by the priest, who claims that the wine is changed into blood in a mysterious way by his touch, etc. This is why Rev. 17:5 says the woman (pope and his church) had "MYSTERY" and "ABOMINATIONS" written in her forehead, which means in her mind or thoughts.

Now let us go on with the remainder of the pope's decree of blasphemy, wherein he claims to be God, etc. I had to break into the middle of it with this explanation to show how clearly St. John described the monster beast with seven heads and its robes of purple, scarlet, silk, decked with precious stones, etc., which the pope, in his writings boasts of having, but never even suspicioning that he is the identical creature described by St. John in his book of Revelation, wherein John says the beast would have a peculiar mouth, speaking great swelling words of blasphemy and wearing purple, scarlet, silk, diamonds, pearls, precious stones, etc., and having "MYSTERY" in his forehead (mind) about that wine turning to blood as a *new* sacrifice to take the place of Christ, Who is our *constant* sacrfice forever and at *all* times. Now let the pope go on with his peculiar mouth and great swelling words issued by him as a message to the world as follows:

> For to me pertaineth first the imperial city of Rome. My daily revenues, my first fruits, indulgences, confessionals, testaments, dispensations, privileges, elections, religious houses, and such like, which come to no small mass of money. The whole world is my diocese, and all men are bound to believe. Wherefore, as I began, so I conclude.

commanding, declaring, and pronouncing, to stand upon *necessity of salvation, for every human creature to be subject to me.*

According to the above decree no one can have even a show of salvation except through the pope at Rome. Here is where he is using that peculiar mouth and swelling words to blaspheme against the Most High, just as St. John declared the beast or harlot *would do.*

And there was given unto him a mouth speaking great things and blasphemies; and power to continue forty-two months.—Rev. 13:5.

Thus we see that he was to have control of the earth 42 months. 42 months at 30 days to each month would make 1260 days. That is, this beast (Roman church) was to come on and run out and smother the true church of Christ, which is called (in this case) a woman, because Christ's *true* church is His bride. This bride of Christ (His church) was to suffer violence from this beast (Roman church) so that she (the Christ bride) would have to run away and hide 1260 days (years).

And the woman fled into the wilderness, where she hath a place prepared for her by God, that they should feed her there 1260 days.—Rev. 12:6.

In my No. 3 book, called OUR NEAR FUTURE, I have shown that 1260 is the same thing as *"a time, times and half a time,"* as mentioned by the prophet Daniel, who also describes how this beast would come on and scatter and break down the Christly church *"a time, times and half a time,"* which means 1260 years.

He sware by Him that liveth that it shall be for a time, times and half a time. And when he (the beast, Roman church) shall have accomplished to scatter the power of the holy people (Christ's church) all these things shall be finished.—Daniel 12:7.

In the No. 3 book, which treats on other and different branches of Bible subjects, it is shown how it is that the Bible calls 360 years a *"time,"* so that *one* "time" is 360, and two more *"times"* are 720, and a *half* a "time" is half of 360, which is 180. Now add these together, 360, 720, 180=1260 years, which is exactly the same as 42 months of 30 days each, which makes 1260 *days*. Raise each day to a year as the prophet Ezekiel declares.

> I have laid upon thee the years of their iniquity, according to the number of the days. I have appointed thee each day for a year.—Ezek. 4:5, 6.

Therefore, the 42 months of 30 days each (making 1260 days) are to mean 1260 *years*, as each day is to be a year. Therefore, when St. John, in his great revelation, declared that the seven-headed beast (meaning the city of Rome on seven hills and the Catholic popes therein) was to continue in power 42 months he meant 1260 years, as the above figures show that 42 months are 1260 *days;* and the prophet Ezekiel comes in and instructs us that each day means a year. And we have the further evidence (calculated and explained in the No. 3 book on another subject) that a *"time,"* as mentioned in the Bible, means 360. Sometimes it is 360 days, while at *other* times (*on other cases*) it is 360 *years*. And St. John says that the "woman" (meaning Christ's church or bride) had to run out in the wilderness and hide away from the monstrous seven-headed beast (Roman church) *"a time, times and half a time."* This makes *one "time"*—two more *"times"* and a *half* of one *"time,"* which, added together, makes three and a half *"times"*; and if 360 is a *"time,"* multiply it (360) by three and one-half and it will make 1260.

And the woman (Christ's church or bride) fled into the wilderness, where she had a place prepared for her by God, that they should feed her there a thousand two hundred and sixty days.—Rev. 12:6.

And as each day means a year, she was to be hid away and smothered out by the (Roman beast) 1260 years, during all of which time the beast was to cut and slash and behead the true followers of Christ, called saints.

And it was given unto him (the Roman beast) to make war with the saints (true followers of Christ) and to overcome them. And power was given him over all kindreds and tongues and nations; and all that dwell upon the earth shall worship him (the Roman beast).—Rev. 13:7, 8.

I have, in previous pages, shown that the dragon (devil) arose from his seat and gave it over to this beast and told it to run things as he (the devil) would run them; and history shows that this Roman beast carried out the devil's instructions to the very letter. This is why it murdered and tortured the folowers of Christ and made war with them and overcame them, just as St. John says it *would* do. It takes the seat of Christ and *pretends* to hand out salvation and forgiveness of sins, and creates a new sacrifice of its own by using that golden cup full of *"abominations."* That is, filling the cup with wine and pretending, by some mysterious hocus-pocus, to change the wine into actual blood and drinking it as a *new* sacrifice and setting aside Christ's sacrifice, which was to last forever. St. John gives a careful outline as to what will befall this Roman beast; and the time is drawing near for it and all its young ones to meet their fate. The Protestant churches (*all* of them) are slivers split off from the Roman beast and they had to come onto earth to hold the world from going headlong into the *"pit,"* as the

Roman beast was pushing things down that GENERAL WORLD HALL, set out in the Pryamid, as pictured in this book. By turning to the picture you will see that the hall ceases to slant at a point 1550 inches this side of the Birth of Christ Point. And if each inch in the hall represents a year, the meaning of it is that 1550 years after the birth of Christ the world would turn or cease to go on down into further darkness. Right there, at that turn in the hall (1550 years after Christ's birth), is where the present Protestant churches stepped on the earth to hold the world from going on down. The Roman beast lost its grip on the people at that point, as I have heretofore shown, and Protestantism sprang up and began to make inroads through the Catholic world. By this we see, as before stated, that the present Protestant church system is only about 350 years old. They *imagine* that they have been in existence ever since the time of the apostles and that they are simply the continuation of the Apostolic church, but it is all *imagination* with them. They are, as I have stated, simply the chips which flew off from the old Roman beast, commonly called the Roman Catholic church; and this is why she is called the Mother of Harlots; and these Protestant churches are the young harlots. This is why they are called *Protestant*. They split off and *protested* against some of the ways of the Roman church. They were *Pro-test-ants*. And this *protesting* commenced about 1550 A. D.—right where the turn in the Pyramid hall is shown. The present churches are no more like the Christly church of the apostles than a cocoanut shell is like a cocoanut. The shell *looks* like a cocoanut, but the meat is lacking and it will deceive you if you are not on the look-out; and this is why I am showing up church history so that people will no longer be deceived by them. They know nothing *at all* about spiritual things. If you talk to them about spiritual power, such as healing the sick and getting revelations from God, they become fighting mad and call you bad names and want to jail you or kill you. They never lose an opportunity to strike at anything spiritual. I have on my desk, at this writing, a church paper which has a large circulation, and it strikes against spiritual healing and all other kinds of spiritual things. Yet it is the regular authorized church paper and the *only* one belonging to the entire denomination in the United States; and all the writers for it claim that their denomination is the only real genuine Apostolic church. They claim it continually and *boldly*, and yet they fight with a vengence against all of the valuable doctrine of Jesus, Whose whole gospel is powerfully spiritual and teaches that we must come into actual communication with God and get revelations and visions from Him and let Him be our King in every little detail; and that we must lay hands on the sick and heal them, and raise the dead and remove mountains and subdue all things. Instead of upholding all this grand doctrine of Jesus we find these churches teaching that the day of miracles is past and you can never get anything from God; and that God has gone away so that no man can ever find Him. If such trash is Apostolic teaching, then these churches are Apostolic as they claim to be. You see they leave out Christ's teachings and manufacture a gospel of their own like their old mother (Roman church) does when she forgives sins and creates new blood for a new sacrifice of their own manufacture and sets Christ aside. Do you see the similarity between these young harlots and their old mother? The world has now arrived at the point where the old mother harlot (Roman church) and all her young ones (Protestant churches) must go down, and be thrown away so that we may know the true God and His Christ and get revelations and power from Him and subdue the world and overcome death and gain victory over it and be Royal High Priests of the great spiritual King. The Protestant churches have accomplished that for which they were sent, and the world now demands a *higher* spiritual church and it will come. It is now on the way, but it will not be the old churches made over or reformed. No, no. Christ tells us that it is not proper to put new wine into old bottles. The old bottles must be thrown away and new bottles for the new wine must come on. They are now being prepared. The filling is taking place. When they are full they will step out as a new nation to rule the world and take charge of all religious, political and social affairs. The old bottles will be no more. The old mother harlot and all her young ones will be obliterated. The old mother held her full time of 1,260 years and used her peculiar mouth and great swelling words with such cunning effect as to deceive the whole world and entrap it. And it fixed up such a fine scheme of doctrine that it worked the greater part of the human family under its clutches so as to get large sums of money out of the people, until it became the most gigantic financial concern on earth. It (the pope and his church) owned country after country and gold, diamonds, jewels, silver and piles and stacks of all kinds of material wealth. But how did the beast get hold of all this wealth? you will ask. Ah, here is the secret golden cup filled with *"abominations,"* as St. John calls it. You know the Bible tells us that the beast would prosper and become mighty and gather unto itself such power as to overcome the followers of Christ and wear them out, and this beast set itself to gaining financial power. It formulated a doctrine and taught it to the people that the pope had power to forgive sins and he (in the aforesaid mentioned decree) declares it openly and notoriously that popes can change times and laws and set aside *"the precepts of Christ."* After a few generations of this teaching the whole public believed it, as the beast would not allow any other kind of teaching. When all the people came to thoroughly believing this abominable teaching it gave a terrible and dreadful advantage into the hands of the pope and he used it for every cent there was in it. He gave out the decree that he could grant *Indulgences* to people. That is, he could remit Purgatorial penalties. Of course the whole public rushed to him to get their religious *"titles clear"* through that awful ordeal of Purgatory. But, hold on. Do you think so great a benefit could be dished out for nothing? Not a bit of it. The income from these sales of Indulgences was *enormous*—beyond all human imagination. People would rake up every cent on the premises to pay for help through Purgatory after death. Henry IV. of Castile received, in four years, as profit on Indulgences, ONE HUNDRED MILLION DOLLARS. This was only a *commission* on the amount and not the amount itself. The pope, as head over the church, would contract with the kings over the governments to allow them a *commission* on sales of Indulgences, etc. The kings would traffic with the pope for *his* favors by paying to him large sums of money to have him issue "religious" orders to the people to make them submissive to the government. This kept the people in the traces so they could be managed. Kings would pay heavily for this out of the taxes collected from the people *themselves*. Then the pope would come in and fleece them on a "religious" charge to pay him for *Indulgences* issued to them to help them out of their sins. Kings could do nothing with the people without the pope's aid, as they (the whole public) looked upon the pope as God, and they would obey the *pope* and let the kings go. This brought hundreds of millions and *billions* of dollars to the pope, as kings were at his mercy. Another scheme which brought much money to the pope was the sale of Privileges. You remember the above decree of the pope declares that he has power to set aside anything he desires and change times and laws, and whenever anything arises that conflicts with his wishes he strikes it down. If the law says that persons shall not marry their cousins or close relatives the pope sets the law aside and issues a Privilege to the person, provided that a large sum of money be paid to the pope for doing this. This scheme brought in great riches. It is reported that a certain person in Italy desired to marry his niece, just recently, but the law was against it, so he paid the pope twenty thousand dollars to get him to set the law aside in this particular case. The Catholic church has a regular list of fees for doing certain things. So much for baptism and so much for saying masses and so on clear through the list. The Roman Catholics teach that when a person dies he goes to Purgatory and that if the priest will say a mass it helps the dead person out of his trouble, and that the more masses that are said the better it is for the dead. This, of course, makes a person rake up all the money he can get and put it in the hands of a priest to pay for masses after the person dies. When you consider the fact that nearly the whole world was under the authority of the Roman church you can then imagine what a great sum of money this scheme brought in, as every body wants to escape punishment, and if you can just make him believe that a pope can bring him through all right the person will pay out his last dollar. The more dollars he pays the more masses he can get; and where a priest is paid a large amount of money for several thousand masses he cannot say them all in a lifetime, therefore, he has to hunt up some poor priest, who lives in an out-of-the-way place, to help him through with these masses. If the original charge for a mass be two dollars he pays the poor priest twenty-five cents for each mass. You will remember that not long ago a certain woman of Spain paid over to the church a sufficient amount of money to pay for five thousand masses for herself and five thousand for her husband.

In addition to these schemes, rich Catholic people will all their property to the church to get masses said over them when dead. The priests and popes permit their members to keep money which they get unlawfully, *provided* that a part of the money be paid to the church. Mr. I. J. Lansing, who has given the Catholic schemes much study, says: "I find that moneys obtained for false witness, for cheating in gambling, for cheating in weights and measures, and money obtained under false pretenses, and money made at prostitution, and many other things are permitted by the church to be kept, *provided* the persons who made these unlawful gains would pay a part of the money to the church. This is so well substantiated that it is beyond doubt or question." This brings in a large pile of money also. Another scheme to get money is by selling certain articles, which Catholics claim have wonderful powers. There is a long list of these articles. Some time ago a Catholic priest wrote in a New York paper that it is right to sell these things on account of the great good they do. He claims that one of these Catholic medals put in watering troughs will keep cattle from getting sick, and that if one of the medals be carried by a person it will protect that person from sickness and from storms and accidents and will even keep away death. A certain priest, whom I could name, gained several hundred thousand dollars by selling these trinkets. You can buy them by the hundred in Catholic stores, which make a specialty of keeping them, and they bring in thousands and millions of dollars. This is why St. John says the merchants will mourn for the beast when she is destroyed from the face of the earth. They will not then have any trinkets to sell to the dupes. Nobody will buy them.

And the merchants of the earth shall mourn over her (the beast), for no man buyeth their merchandise any more.—Rev. 18:11.

The people of this country (United States) have not the slightest knowledge of this monstrous animal (the seven-headed Roman beast) and the wonderful schemes and pretensions it puts forth to deceive and fleece the people. This is why St. John declares that all nations were deceived by it.

By thy sorceries were all nations deceived and in her (the old mother harlot) was found the blood of prophets and of saints and of all that were slain upon the earth.—Rev. 18:23, 24.

When you understand the ways and schemes of the beast and how she sells masses, indulgences, privileges, dispensations and decrees and grows rich from her abominations, and how the pope held the kings of the earth in his grasp so that they would be compelled to pay him large sums of money to induce him to issue decrees to keep the people from rising up against the governments; when you understand all of this you will then see what the book of Revelation is talking about when it mentions the old harlot and how the kings of the earth committed fornication with her, which means that they paid her money to get her to do certain things in their favor.

All nations have drunk of the wine of the wrath of her fornication, and the kings of the earth have committed fornication with her, and the merchants became rich through her delicacies (*that is, they sold her goods and trinkets which she taught* the people were necessary for their welfare).—Rev. 18:3.

Of course these secrets of the church doctrine and her woolly ways are not intended to get out to the general public, but we do get hold of them in various ways, so that our statements are founded on their decrees and books and rules of the church, and it will surprise the people of this country to learn the truth about this beast. Those who desire to look into her history will find the writings of Henry C. Lea, H. G. Guinness, I. J. Lansing, Dr. McGlynn and others of great value, and it would pay the people well to investigate this subject, as it will throw much light on Bible statements and will also show why the beast is the mother of harlots, as it will be seen that the present Protestant churches were born out of her and that they carry her ear-marks and ways and many of her false ideas, and that the only way for the genuine Christian to gain the true spiritual God is to cut loose from all the churches now on earth and have nothing at all to do with them, as they are, in many respects, the deadly enemy of God, and no one can mix in with them without becoming more or less tainted with their evil ideas and teachings. While it is true that the Protestant churches are an improvement on the old mother beast, and they have done much toward breaking her back (just as God designed that they should) yet they, the Protestant churches of to-day, are not at all fit or competent to lead the people to that high and grand spiritual power of the Holy Ghost, who will show us visions and talk with us and give us power to heal the sick, raise the dead, remove mountains and do all things. All these things are open and ready for us, but we never can gain them by following the methods and teachings of the present church system, as every one of them thoroughly believes and *teaches* that "the day of miracles is past" and that it is not possible for us, in this day, to do the wonderful things that Jesus and the apostles did, although Jesus *himself* declares that we shall and *must* do greater things than ever *He* did, but the churches of to-day give the *lie* right to His face by teaching us that it cannot be done, and they use every effort to keep the people from believing anything of the kind, and when we *insist* upon it they say that we are teaching spiritism and that we are possessed of the devil, and all this kind of stuff. They use *exactly* the same argument that the churches used against Jesus when He was here on earth. They said He was possessed of the devil and that He was casting out sickness by the power of a big devil spirit which they called Beelzebub. If they slandered *Him* and used their mouths against the Perfect and Holy One (Christ Jesus), what can a *common* personage like I expect from them? The world has come to the point where it must go up higher spiritually, and to do this it must cut down and destroy the old errors; and this process always causes daggers in the air, as error is always popular and has the great majority on its side, so that whoever draws his butcher-knife against it has the entire public to fight, so that nothing but the powerful spiritual sword of the Most High can stand against it, but His whizzing sickle is abundantly able to cut down the multitude, and on this I rely. I have pointed out the beast. Have shown his number to be 666. I have shown you her blasphemous mouth that utters great swelling words against the Most High. I have shown to you her fornications and sorceries and only a *few* of her many schemes, which have deceived the whole earth. To show *all* of her cunning sales and practices would make this book too large and expensive to reach the people; therefore, I now turn my attention to the *clothes* of the beast, in order to identify him, as he was to wear certain kinds and colors of garments. Let us now examine them. But you will say, What does all this have to do with the Pyramid? I am showing why the General World Hall slants downward and runs into the dark pit, underground. The "beast," now under consideration, was given the devil's seat and authority and killed the followers of the true God and led off, downward, into darkness of the pit;

and to understand this mighty subject you must know who and what the beast is; and for this purpose we are identifying him by looking at his number (666) and his mark and his mouth and his high titles and pretensions. Now we will examine his clothes and showy trinkets. It will be noticed that all the way through, the prophets and the Apostle John describe it as a *beast* and a prostitute; and this is why they apply the name "Scarlet Woman" to it. Notice how accurately the pope's dress and fixtures are described.

> I saw a woman (prostitute) sit upon a scarlet colored beast, full of names of blasphemy, having seven heads (seven hills of Rome), and the "woman" was arrayed in purple and scarlet color and decked with gold and precious stones and pearls, having a golden cup in her hand, full of abominations and filthiness of her fornications; and upon her forehead (in his mind) was a name written. MYSTERY, BABYLON THE GREAT, THE MOTHER OF HARLOTS AND ABOMINATIONS OF THE EARTH. And the woman (city of Rome and the pope) were drunken with the blood of the martyrs of Jesus.—Rev. 17.

You will notice that the above prophecy declares that the "woman" (meaning the pope, who sells decrees and favors for money) would be dressed in *purple*, scarlet, etc., etc., decked with gold and precious stones, etc. If you have ever attended high mass or solemn high mass or any great pow-wow in the large Catholic cathedrals you will be forced to remember St. John's vision of the dress and ornaments the "beast" would wear, as the whole prophecy is acted out to the very letter. I have watched it. The cardinals, bishops, priests and high officers of the church, dressed in their magnificent robes of many colored silks, braids, etc., come out before the audience and use that peculiar mouth, which we have just discussed, in blasphemy against the Most High.

Just now the papers bring us the account of the in-inauguration of a new cardinal. The ceremony took place here in the United States and the Catholics marched in procession with great display and the daily papers, in describing it, have something to say about the rich dress and robes of the high officers of the church. I clip from the papers a little of it, that you may see, in *actual* operation, what St. John saw in *vision* about the purple, gold, scarlet, etc., which the beast would wear. Here is what the papers say of the parade.

CHURCH DIGNITARIES IN PROCESSION.

After these came about fifty bishops and a score or more of archbishops, the purple and gold of their rich vestments glistening in the cold, clear air, their immense trains held up by little boys, in brilliant vestments. Upon his shoulders hung the beautiful cloak of cardinal silk and ermine. Half a dozen train-bearers clad in cardinal velvet and gilt braid followed in his wake.

As further comment on the identification of the pope and his great blasphemous organization being the "Scarlet Woman," the "Harlot," the "Beast," etc., mentioned in Revelation, as wearing purple, gold, precious stones and speaking great things against the Most High, I now introduce the account of a great convention of high Roman dignitaries, held in Rome, in July, 1870 A. D., and at which meeting they framed a decree that the pope was infallible, which means that he can not err, but that he is always right in all things, the same as God. After voting this decree through, they set a day when they would have a big *pow-wow* over it and declare it *publicly* before all the world. Dr. Cummings, of England, describes the big demonstration at Rome as follows:

The pope had a grand throne erected in front of the eastern window in St. Peter's, and arrayed himself in a perfect blaze of precious stones, and surrounded himself with cardinals and patriarchs and bishops in gorgeous apparel for a magnificent spectacular scene. He had chosen the early morning hour and the eastern window,—that the rising sun should flash its beams full upon his magnificence, and by it his diamonds, rubies and emeralds (see how his dress fits the description of Rev. 17:4 and Rev. 18:16) be so refracted and reflected that he should appear to be not a man, but what the decree proclaimed him, one having all the glory of God. The pope posted himself at an early hour at the eastern window, but the sun refused to . . . shine. The dismal dawn darkened rapidly to a deeper and deeper gloom. The dazzle of glory could not be produced. The aged eyes of the would be God could not see to read by daylight, and he had to send for candles. Candle-light strained his nerves of vision too much, and he handed the reading over to a cardinal. The cardinal began to read amid an ever blackening gloom, but had not read many lines before such a glare of lurid fire and such a crash burst from the inky heavens as was never equaled at Rome before. Terror fell upon all. The reading ceased. One cardinal jumped trembling from his chair, and exclaimed, "It is the voice of God speaking, the thunders of Sinai."

Having identified the great "beast" and his peculiar mouth speaking great things and blaspheming against the Most High, by applying to himself the titles *"Ruler of the Universe," "Holy Father of Fathers," "King of Heaven, Earth and Hell"* and many other high names belonging to none but God; and having found his number (666), and his *mark*, made with ashes, crossed on the forehead; and having examined his clothes (robes) with the purple, scarlet, gold, precious stones and other trimmings; and his great riches and prosperity, as mentioned by St. John, the next question is to find his *location*. Where was he to dwell on earth? St. John's vision answers the question, by telling us that the "beast" or "harlot" would live in a city, which would sit on seven hills or knobs or mountains, and Rome is just such a location, as she sits on seven hills.

The prophet saw ten horns coming out of the seven heads. These horns were kings ruling the provinces round about. Now notice that *"horn"* means king. Now go back and read the prophecy, quoted herein, and see how another *"little horn"* sprang up *among* the ten. That little horn was the *beginning* of the RomanCatholic pope and his church —a mere speck at first—just a little "horn" or king over a small *church* organization. It began to germinate, 100 years after Christ's resurrection, and it ran along, gathering power, over 400 years more, and, finally, hatched out, with its center (pope) on the seven hills of Rome (seven heads) and took possession of the earth, so that all the kings had to bow down to it and get its consent before taking any action on any thing. This caused the kings to make leagues with and bribes to the pope to get his influence in carrying out their bold schemes to hamper the people and bleed them. The pope and his church would favor any body or any thing for gain—just like any other prostitute, and this is why the New Testament calls it the great harlot. Kings had to buy favors from it or else lose their position and also their heads. This was all shown to Saint John in the vision, 500 years before it took place.

> And one of the seven angels talked with me, saying: Come, and I will shew thee the judgment of the great whore that sitteth upon many waters—and with whom the kings of the earth have committed fornication, and the inhabitants of the earth have been made drunk (disorderly and reckless) with the wine of her fornication.—Rev. 17.

Not only kings had to bribe it with money and presents to get favors from it, but every merchant and business man was boycotted and made come to time. And if the merchant or any other man, after being boycotted and starved out, still refused to agree with the "beast," orders went out to kill the man.

That as many as would not worship the image of the beast *should be killed.*—Rev. 13:15.

Saint John foresaw just how the beast would work it by slaughtering men who insisted on holding to Christ and His teachings. The beast beheaded them.

I saw under the altar the souls of them that were slain for the word of God and for the testimony (belief) which they held.—Rev. 6:9.

The *desperate* tortures and slaughter which this beast inflicted on all who would not agree with it is beyond the power of words to describe. It hung on so many hundred years (1,260 years) and became so extremely vicious and murderous, that the souls of those who were butchered looked out from under the altar and in great agony cried unto God to stop it.

And they cried with a loud voice, saying, How long, O Lord, dost thou not judge and avenge our blood on them that dwell on earth?—Rev. 6:10.

With these preludes and explanations I now bring forth the testimony of St. John, in his own words, as to the *place* where the "beast," "harlot" or "woman" or "666" man would make his or her headquarters. Rev. 17 speaks as follows:

VERSE 18. The *woman* is that great city (city of Rome) which reigneth over the kings of the earth. VERSE 9. The seven heads are seven mountains on which the woman (city of Rome) sitteth. VERSE 15. The waters where the whore sitteth are peoples, multitudes, nations and tongues. VERSE 12. The ten horns are ten kings.

Babylon means confusion. The pope and his church had turned Christ's teachings upside down and twisted them all out of their proper meaning and filled in their own doctrine, which came from the dragon (devil), as the scripture heretofore quoted says that the dragon (devil) gave his own seat to the beast (pope) and turned over all his power to the beast (the pope) and told him to run things as he himself (the devil) would run it, and the pope and his many successors *did* run it with a *vengeance* and slaughtered every body and every thing who held to the Christly way. This is why the scripture above quoted says that the city of Rome and the pope were drunken with the blood of the followers of Jesus. Rev. 18 describes the desperate wickedness of this beast (the Roman church), sometimes called Babylon on account of the terrible confusion which it caused. The very worst elements of society took shelter in it. This was clearly shown to Saint John in his vision.

I saw an angel come down from heaven, and he cried with a strong voice, saying, Babylon (Roman Church) is become the habitation of devils and every foul spirit, and is a cage for every unclean and hateful thing; for all nations have drunk of the wine of her fornication, and the kings of the earth have committed fornication with her. (Paid her money for favors in helping them with their schemes.) Come out of her, my people, that ye be not partakers of her sins, and that ye receive not of her plagues; for her sins have reached unto heaven. Her plagues shall come in a day, death and mourning and famine, and she shall be utterly burned with fire.—Rev. 18.

The lines are now being formed to sweep her from the earth—not leaving a speck of her. The great beast is on its last legs. It has carried on high carnival and soaked itself in the blood of the followers of Christ about 1,500 years, 1,260 of which it had *full* possession of the earth and ran the people down into the most vile and ignorant condition, so that scarcely any one could read or write. They marauded around and reveled in murder, rapine and blood. They made war on the saints (followers of Christ) and wore them out and beheaded them. The pope set himself up as the successor of Saint Peter, and as such pretended to hold the keys to the Kingdom of God, as set out in Matt. 16:18, 19, as follows:

And Jesus said: Thou art Peter, and upon this rock I will build *my* church and the gates of hell shall not prevail against it; and I will give to thee the keys of the kingdom of heaven, and whatsoever thou shalt bind on earth shall be bound in heaven, and whatsoever thou shalt loose on earth shall be loosed in heaven.

This idea was taught to the people, and children were born and raised under it during all that long and dreadful period of 1,500 years, so that every one thoroughly believed that whatever the pope said had to be done, as he held those keys to the kingdom of heaven and he could *bind* you or loose you at his own sweet will; and that to disobey orders was disobeying God. And the pope claimed that he was in *constant* communication with St. Peter and that all the pope's orders were *direct* from Peter. And all the world believing this gave the pope complete authority over kings and every body. He had his bishops and his priests stationed in every neighborhood throughout Europe, and whenever a person refused to worship the "beast" (the pope and the church) he was reported to headquarters, and orders would come back to *kill* him; and as nearly every one regarded the orders as *direct* from God, the whole neighborhood would *gladly* execute the orders with *intense* delight. They regarded the pope and the church as the kingdom of God, and the church *taught* this continually. It was a great way for the kingdom of God to act; murder, torture and slaughter people. But perhaps you are wondering again what all this argument has to do with the Pyramid. As heretofore stated, I am showing what caused the *General World Hall* to slant *downward* towards the "pit" (the dark room in the earth). It will be remembered that the hall was in direct line with' and pointed to the *dragon* star. It was the road of the *dragon* (devil). It will also be remembered that the *dragon* (the devil) arose from his seat and gave it to the beast with seven heads (city of Rome on seven hills and the pope located therein); and it has been shown that the pope sat down in the devil's seat, with the devil's authority and ran things in the ground in the most horrible manner, so that the world became ignorant and dark and *"beastly"* vicious. The people were on the downward road to the "pit," under ground. God is symbolized in scripture as the sun, on account of the brilliant light thrown off from Him or by Him. The *people* of the earth are represented as the *moon*, on account of the reflection of light. The great beast (the pope and his church) were like an eclipse, which prevented the light of the sun (God) from shining. Now notice that St. John, in his vision, saw what black darkness the *beast* would spread over the earth and how it would shut off the light of God (Sun) and murder the people (moon) so that their blood would flow freely every where before all eyes.

And I beheld, when he had opened the sixth seal the sun (God) became black (out of sight) and the moon (people) became as blood.—Rev. 6:12.

The general public is not at all acquainted with

the bloody history of the monstrous beast or harlot. There is much more to be said on this subject, but enough has been shown to give a reason for the downward slant of the hall in the Pyramid. As heretofore explained, Martin Luther and others broke in against the "beast" and began to start a reformation, and, finally, Napoleon Bonaparte came onto the earth (for an express purpose); and he was a man who cared nothing for God, man nor the devil. He took the bit in his mouth and roamed over the earth and trampled everything down, according to his own sweet will, and declared himself Dictator and held possession, and drove kings, princes and potentates off their thrones and appointed his own relatives and friends to take their places.

He made the pope and his church dance to the music of the dagger, and, finally, seized the pope and put him in prison and kept him there till the pope died. This shocked the people of earth as though an earthquake had struck them. The idea that any *man* would have the audacity to "tackle" god and put him in jail was stunning; as many generations had been born and brought up under the *constant* teaching that the pope was God, or, rather, the successor of Saint Peter, and, as such, held the keys to the kingdom of heaven; and no one but Napoleon would ever *think* of crossing the will of the pope, much less seize him and put him behind the bars. But Napoleon cared nothing for that kind of a god or any other God, and he just went right on cutting and slashing the church and its high officers and everything at his pleasure. This opened the people's eyes a little and broke the "spell" that had been hovering over them nearly 1500 years. They began to see that the pope could *not* call down the wrath of heaven against any one who refused to do the pope's will, and the people, finally, rose up and began to slash the church and behead the bishops and priests and confiscate their property in a general mad scramble, so that the Catholic kings, priests, officers and members had to "take to the woods" and hide, to escape the mad wrath of the public. This terrible slaughter and confiscation lasted twenty-five years (from 1789 to 1815 A. D.). Words cannot describe it. History calls it the French Revolution.

The kings of the earth, and the great men, and the rich men, and the chief captains, and the mighty men, and every bond man, and every free man, hid themselves in dens and in rocks of the mountains; and said to the mountains and rocks, Fall on us and hide us from the wrath of the Lamb (Christ).—Rev. 6:15, 16.

The beast with seven heads (Rome and the church) had been slaughtering the followers of Christ and carrying on highway robbery and murder during all its allotted time of 1260 years (a time, times and half a time. See Daniel 12:7 and Rev. 12:14. As to the explanation of this and how it is calculated, see my No. 3 book, entitled *Our Near Future*); and the souls of those beheaded looked out from under the altar and cried unto God, "How long, O Lord, how long dost thou not avenge our blood on them that dwell on earth?" and vengeance came onto the pope, bishops, priests, members, city, country, property, and every thing; and Napoleon put the cap-sheaf on it by putting the pope in jail and keeping him there. The pope had been the supreme ruler over not only the church, all over Europe, but also ruler over all kings and governments; and such a *terrible* disaster as the public and Napoleon heaped upon the beast broke its back-bone. It lost its power and has been dwindling down with spinal disease ever since, so that *now* it is a very weak thing, compared to what it *used* to be, when it ruled the earth and chewed up every body and every thing with its iron teeth.

Its fall and disappearance goes on *gradually*, and by spells, the same as was its rise and growth. While it was *coming* on the earth, circumstances combined to push it upward into power; and after it had held possession its allotted time of 1260 years, circumstances began to combine *against* it to destroy it. Martin Luther and others hit it a stunning blow *religiously*; then Napoleon stabbed it politically and every way. Then Garibaldi came on and struck it another hard lick, September 20, 1870, by declaring that the pope (thereafter) must keep his hand out of government matters. Then King Victor Emmanuel of Italy said something similar to the pope; King Humbert also refused to hand back to the "Holy Father" (as the pope is called) any authority to rule over government. Thus the "Holy Father" finds himself cut off all around, and he thinks it is an outrage. He holds to the idea that he should be not only the head of the *church*, but the head of the governments also; and after Garibaldi cut off the power of the pope, the "Holy Father" issued an order that all Catholics should enter into politics and labor to have the constitutions and laws changed so as to restore the old-timed authority to him (the pope and the church). This would put all the governments of earth in the control of the Roman pope; and to prevent this, an organization called the *American Protective Association* (known as the A. P. A.), was formed in the United States. Its chief aim is to prevent

Catholics from being elected to any offices, and by this means offset the efforts and orders of the pope. This A. P. A. organization is already becoming a mighty influence in elections, as is shown by the following interview, which I clip from the Kansas City *Star* of September 23, 1895:

MILLIONS IN THE A. P. A.

Startling Claims of the Order's National Vice-President.

The Society Will Go into National Politics Next Year and Will Cast Its Whole Strength with the Party That Favors Its Principles.

J. H. Jackson of Fort Worth, Tex., national vice-president of the American Protective Association, came to Kansas City last night and will lecture at Turner Hall to-night. When asked about the condition of the A. P. A., he said:

"The order is growing rapidly in numbers. We are getting the conservative men, the very best class of citizens, now. People who a year or two ago would not talk with us about joining the order are coming to us now. We have in round numbers 3½ million members. In California we have 200,000 and in the older States farther east the number of members we have is enormous and growing daily. We won't vote with a party that condemns our principles, and we won't support any party that makes a bid for the Roman Catholic vote. We will take hold with whoever wants to join us in securing honest men in office and men who place their loyalty to the United States above their allegiance to any pope, prince or potentate or any other power on earth. Under our form of government too much liberty is enjoyed for the pope to rule the actions of the people. Who brought on this fight? Why, the Catholics. Pope Leo issued an order in 1885 that all Catholics should labor as far as possible to have the constitutions of the States framed in accordance with the laws of the church and that Catholics should enter into politics everywhere. They say we began this fight, but we didn't. The A. P. A. was organized in 1887 and Pope Leo issued his order in 1885."

Thus we see that the gun is being loaded again to fire at the seven-headed beast with the peculiar mouth, speaking blasphemy against the Most High;

and the beast sees this and is making a desperate effort to run into a safe place of its own so that it can stand with its back to the wall and prevent the pursuers from running in behind it and firing from the rear, as the following clipping from London to the New York *World* shows:

TO BUY ROME FOR THE POPE.

A Circular Issued to Catholics Proposing the Plan.

Bankrupt Italy Might Surrender the Eternal City for a Ransom of One Billion Dollars, and the Temporal Power Might Thus be Restored.

London, Sept. 16.—Somewhat over a month ago the *World* published from here a cabled synopsis of a proposition that had been submitted to leading Roman Catholics in Europe to take advantage of the serious financial difficulties in Italy and raise a fund for purchasing Rome, with the idea of re-establishing the temporal power of the pope. Nothing less is proposed than that the Catholic countries and peoples of the world should combine to ransom Rome. To those familiar with the organization and the working of the Roman Catholic communion, and with the intensity of desire which animates the Catholic church to secure the perfect independence of its spiritual head, it would not be difficult to believe that if the scheme is once set on foot a large sum of money may be collected and placed in the hands of Leo XIII.

Cardinal Satolli, a direct agent of the pope, and now in the United States, was interviewed on the subject, and the newspapers represent him as saying as follows:

The Holy Father regards the Italian king as an usurper, and as one who unlawfully withholds that which belongs to the representative of Christ, and, as such, it would be beneath his high and lofty position to make any overtures whatever. There has been some discussion in certain political circles of asking the Italian government to sell to a committee appointed for that purpose, a certain part of Rome, known as the Lenine city, and it was proposed to deed it to the present Holy Father and to his successors as a private estate entailed on their office. This section includes the great Vatican and its magnificent gardens, the castle of San Angelo and the church of St. Peter. The agitators of it are not inclined to ask that the pope be granted any small principality, nor anything less than the whole of the confiscated papal possessions."

And thus the ball rolls on for trouble and death to the beast, but it is trying to stand against it.

September 20, 1870, was the date when Garibaldi took away the temporal or political power of the pope and it is made a holiday by the anti element and is observed each year by celebrations and parades. The last one caused the factions to become angry, and general disturbance was the result. The Catholics regard the celebrations as an outrage, and they protest in bitter words and actions.

New York, Sept. 21.—Archbishop Corrigan has forwarded to Pope Leo XIII. a beautifully illuminated parchment on which is inscribed an address by the German Catholics of New York to the Holy Father. It begins by alluding to the blessings of religious freedom enjoyed by Catholics in this country and protests solemnly, "before the face of the whole world, against the sacrilegious violation done to the patrimony of St. Peter in September, 1870." It is bound in vellum and inclosed in an elaborate and expensive case, carefully wrapped in canvas and wood before shipment to-day.

Thus we see that the seven-headed beast dies hard; but that it will die *completely* is positively certain, as it was shown to St. John the revelator and is fully described in the 17th and 18th chapters of Revelation, part of which has already come to pass and the remainder will follow, but, trouble first.

In reading the brief extract which I copy from those two chapters, you must remember that the *woman* mentioned there means the city of Rome, where the pope has always resided and ruled over the earth.

> The woman is that great city, which reigneth over the kings of earth.—Rev. 17:18.

And the beast with seven heads is also the city of Rome and the pope and his church. Rome, remember, sits on seven high knobs or hills.

> The seven heads are seven mountains on which the woman (city) sitteth.—Rev. 17:9.

It must also be remembered that the *"Babylon"* mentioned there means *confusion*—that is, the city of Rome being the head and center of the Roman Catholic church, *confused* the gospel of Christ and tore it into pieces and turned it around to suit its own purposes, so that now there are hundreds of denominations, and some are teaching just the reverse of the others; no two are alike, yet they all claim to be the mouth-pieces of God. It is a general mixture of all kinds of stuff. No wonder it is called confusion (Babylon) by the Revelator. And the city of Rome (called the woman) was the *starter* of all this confusion of doctrines, and I have heretofore shown that this is why the city (and the pope) are called the *Mother* of Harlots, as all the *present* church organizations sprang out of her, and the Revelator positively proclaims that they are the *young* harlots; while the Roman church is the old *mother* harlot *"full of blasphemy and abominations."* It is conceded by all men that the young ones inherit the traits of character and dispositions of the mother; this being the case, let us just briefly trace the character of the old mother harlot and then see whether the young ones have any similarity to her. Elsewhere in this chapter I have shown how the old mother harlot (the beast with seven heads) ruled the entire earth 1260 years (which is a "time, times and half a time" as mentioned in Rev. 12:14) in *full* control, besides 400 years more of only partial control; and that while she thus ruled she cut and slashed and murdered and burned the followers of Christ and all others who refused to accept her doctrines. Her record is one of blood and terror until Napoleon struck her and Garibaldi struck her and King Emmanuel and King Humbert struck her and made her behave more decently. Now examine her *young* ones. I have much evidence showing that the present Protestant church organizations (the young harlots) are out and after the men who are now teaching the doctrine that Christ is not dead, but alive, and will heal the sick, raise the dead and do as He used to do if we will trust Him. They arrest and imprison these men and run them out of the town and do violence to them, and try to prove them insane, as an excuse to put them in the asylum and shut them up, so as to prevent them from drawing their congregations into this high spiritual faith and trust in God. This trait of character the present Protestant churches inherit from their *mother*, the old harlot, which is the Roman Catholic church, as *she* was always imprisoning and cutting the heads off of those who disagreed with her. I am constantly meeting her young ones (Protestant churches) and they nearly always have anger in their hearts at me for teaching the idea that *they* are not the mouthpieces of God, but that, in *reality*, they are the *enemies* of Christ by trying to strip Him of His power by teaching their congregations that "the day of miracles is past" and that Christ will not heal your bodily afflictions or do any thing for you nowadays. You know the Revelator, in chap. 17:3-7, says the "*mother* harlot" was full of blasphemy and abominable teaching; therefore, it is clear to see where the young ones (Protestant churches) get their blasphemous teaching against Christ. The old *"mother"* harlot is all form and no spirit. She calls her congregation together and goes through a long string of forms, and they count their beads and bow and make signs of the cross, etc., etc., and then adjourn, with the understanding that they have worshiped the Spirit of God. Now look at the young harlots (Protestant churches). They go to church and go through with a set form and adjourn, believing that they have worshiped God too. They go right on grabbing after dollars and indulging in sex relations to their hearts' content and give up nothing nor come close to God to hear His voice to get instructions; indeed they become *very* angry if any one tells them that God will talk to men *these* days. They *rave* and call such teaching "cranky" and arrest the person for teaching it. They want to strip God of His power and make Him a last year's almanac— out of date now, just as their old *"mother"* did when she set the pope up in Christ's place and done away with His sacrifice, which was to last each day forever; so she trampled Christ's daily sacrifice under foot and set up her own abominations that have made the world desolate, so that scarcely any one will allow Christ any power these days. They, all (the church organizations), set Him aside as being out of date.

From the time that the daily sacrifice shall be taken away and the abomination that maketh desolate set up there shall be 1290 years.—Daniel 12:11.

The above time expired some years ago, and this is why the old mother harlot is receiving so many strokes on the head. And her young ones (the Protestant churches) *are* going down with her. Their time is up. They have served their purpose and must step down. They can no longer thrust a bar-rail between Christ and the people by teaching them that "the day of miracles is past." With their *mouths* they draw people towards Christ, but when some earnest soul attempts to use Him to heal sickness or act as King, to guide in little details of life, they sneer such person out of countenance and call him insane, cranky, and other pet names. When brought right down, *face to face* with Christ or no Christ, they fly the track every time and sneer at Him and His power. They *reject* Him. They get this trait of character from their "*mother*," the *old* harlot (the Roman church), who makes *great* ceremony over the cross and such things, but is careful to go to the Virgin Mary or to the pope for help. They set aside Christ's great sacrifice and set up their own abominations in its stead.

The present church organizations of the world are simply the tail end of the "beast," which has its *head* in the great city of Rome, on seven hills; and these tails are switching around all over the earth and drawing people with them and teaching them that Christ has no power *nowadays* and that if He *has* He will not use it for any body or any thing; and when a poor soul denies such teaching and holds up for Christ and His daily power, these tails switch him in the face and blind him and throw him down to the earth. All these persons who are now holding up for Christ's power and are claiming that Christ *will, these days,* act as King and heal, instruct and protect, they are called *"stars of heaven,"* for the reason that they are higher, spiritually, than the general mass of persons. They think and act more in harmony with heaven. Now notice what the Revelator says about the tails of the beast switching these "stars" down.

> And there appeared a great red dragon, having seven heads; and his tail drew the third part of the stars of heaven and cast them down to earth.—Rev. 12:3, 4.

The dragon and his tails have always stood and are now standing, ready to defeat Christ and His power. When the apostles started the *real* church and teachings of Christ, the doctrine was scarcely born before the dragon with seven heads ran in and gobbled it up and tore it in pieces and ran the *real* Christly church out into the wilderness, and made it hide 1260 years. In reading the Revelator's account of it, you must know the word *"woman"* in *this* particular case means the real church of Christ, which was to bring a Christly condition to the people of earth; but the dragon prevented it and killed the starters of it and ran the whole structure out of the country.

> And the dragon stood before the woman (Christ's church) which was ready to be delivered, for to devour her child so soon as it was born. And the woman (church) fled into the wilderness, where she hath a place prepared of God, that they should feed her there (hid) 1260 days (years).—Rev. 12: 4, 6.

And she is just now coming back, out of the wilderness, after having been run out and smothered all these many centuries; and the child is being born. The new and *real* church of Christ is just now being constructed. It is a body of persons called the Elect. You will notice that the Revelator says it was a *red* dragon that ran the Christ church out. *Red* means blood, and blood means murder; therefore, the dragon was to be a murderous concern. This was just what the seven-headed beast was; it slaughtered small and great if they refused to agree with it. *Red* is one of the adopted colors for the dress of the "beast." Here is where the name "cardinal red" came from. The cardinals are high officers, next to the pope, in the Roman church, and their robes are cardinal red; and many other officers in the church must also wear cardinal red while at service. At the inauguration of the cardinal, heretofore mentioned in this chapter, they went through a great pow-wow over a *red* beretta and then placed it on the new cardinal as an emblem or mark to show that he is now cardinal. They never even dreamed that they were fulfilling St. John's revelation about the red dragon. How very accurately the Revelator describes the beast and its dress, even down to colors (see Rev. 17:4), although the vision was shown to St. John hundreds of years before the beast became established on the seven hills of Rome. This all goes to show that it was not a *happen* case. Of course not. *Nothing* happens. The present Protestant church organizations did not just happen. They were permitted to come onto earth to hold the world from going down into the pit. The seven-headed beast was rushing things down, headlong, and the split off from it, called Protestant, became necessary to hold things. The Protestant organizations deserve their reward for holding the world in check and *talking* Christ at the people to prevent them from forgetting Him; and in *this* their labors have not been in vain; but they are *totally* incompetent to teach the people the spiritual side of Christ's Gospel, for the reason that the organizations themselves have no knowledge of God's spiritual laws, and, therefore, they can never lead the world upward. This is shown in the *General World Hall* of the Pyramid, where it ceases to go down on a slant, but turns and runs along on a *level*. This turning of the hall probably represents the work of the Protestant churches, started by Martin Luther and others, about 1550 A. D. After the hall turns it does not run upward, but continues on the same level as it was at the turning point. This is why the Elect, or Royal Body of High Priests, with Christ as their Chief and King and Head must now come on and lead the world *upward*. In using the words "High Priests" they must not be taken to mean such priests as are *now* operating on earth. *Far* from it. I mean a body of persons who are thoroughly spiritualized and understand the spiritual laws and ways of God; persons who received their education entirely from God. They are sealed unto God. Melchizedek was such a person. Christ was an High Priest after the order of Melchizedek. (See Heb. 6:20.) This is the kind of High Priests I mean. God is now preparing them, and when *they* come before the world, the long rejected stone (Christ and His power) will be made the chief cap-stone or top corner stone; the finishing touch; the sharp point at the top of the Pyramid; the pattern showing the angles and slant from which the foundation was laid for the building. During all these many centuries He has been kept back and rejected as having no power nowadays; but the *Elect* will acknowledge Him as the Head of the corner. They will do this not only with their *mouths*, but with their actions, and show to the world that *He* is really King in *fact* and not by name only. This will break down and *totally* destroy all the present church organizations (Protestant and Catholic). But in referring to these organizations, as I have in this chapter, I do it not to slur them or to condemn them, as God *permitted* them to come on earth, and they have performed a purpose and their day is now closing. Their sun is setting. Even a thing so terrible and murderous as the seven-headed beast, God *permitted* it to come, and, through the prophets and St. John, foretold the world that it *would* come; and He even went so far as to describe the robes of cardinal red, purple and scarlet that it would wear; and told us about the tails it would have scattered all over the earth to sweep down the spiritual persons (stars of heaven); and how a great number of young ones (organizations) would spring from it, so that it would be the *mother* of harlots and abominable things generally. (Rev. 17:5.) Therefore, it is plain that the thing did not come by chance; and when it had run its full course, then a terrible man (Napoleon) came on and struck it a paralyzing blow; and history is writing down Napoleon as a bad man generally—a sort of highway robber—destitute of all moral principle; and indeed, the prophet Daniel also described a similar character, thousands of years before Napoleon was born. And he came walking in on time to strike the beast and turn the governments around for a purpose. And then the Protestant churches came on with all their conflicting doctrines and hundreds of denominations, so that there is nothing but confusion and uncertainty every where. It is like the confusion of tongues at the Tower of Babel (Gen. 11).

The *"beast"* had run every thing downward until the time when Martin Luther and others cut across its path and checked its horrible influence; and this was followed by Napoleon, who thrust his dagger into it and let out its blood. In other words, Napoleon extracted its poisonous fangs—just as other rattlesnakes are treated to prevent them from doing injury. It is an operation that a *timid* man would not undertake. Neither would any *ordinary* person start out to throw the halter over the head of the "beast" which had roamed over the earth, devouring every thing in its path 1260 years. But when God's set time came to break the back of the beast there came onto the earth a man with just the right kind of a temper and disposition to do the work. It took a beast to cope with the great "beast," and all writers of history set Napoleon down as having a disposition as near "beastly" as any man ever had.

AN ALL-ROUND BAD MAN.

RALPH WALDO EMERSON'S OPINION OF NAPOLEON THE FIRST.

Bonaparte was singularly destitute of generous sentiments. He was unjust to his generals, egotistic and monopolizing, meanly stealing the credit of their great actions. He was thoroughly unscrupulous. He would steal, slander, assassinate, drown and poison, as his interest dictated. He had no generosity, but mere vulgar hatred; he was intensely selfish; he was perfidious; he cheated at cards; he was a prodigious gossip and opened letters and delighted in his infamous police and rubbed his hands with joy when he had intercepted some morsel of intelligence concerning the men and women about him, boasting that he "knew everything."

Of course he was a desperate man and the condition of the world at that time required just such a character to strike the beast, which had been burning, murdering, beheading and torturing God's followers over 1500 years. The old seven-headed "beast" had a regular organized system of murder built up and officers and agents established over the earth, like spiders, to throw out nets and catch the weary innocent and drag them up to the post and burn them alive. A great office, called the Holy Office, was established to attend to the murdering and torture of all who had not the mark of the beast on them.

The Inquisition or Holy Office, between 1480 and 1809, put to death by burning 31,912; burned in effigy 17,659, and imprisoned 291,450. The massacre of St. Bartholomew was political as well as religious in its motives; by it some 70,000 Huguenots were put to death. In England, Mary I. caused 277 persons to be burned to death, and Elizabeth put to death about 200 priests and put as many more in prison. This is only a "drop in the bucket" when compared to the wholesale slaughter that had been going on, hundreds of years, by direction of the beast with seven heads. Napoleon stepped onto the stage of action and slashed the beast and every body, so that in a short time 9,200 persons were massacred, besides 2,122,402 soldiers were cut down between 1792 and 1804 A. D. The mad dance was going on all over Europe, and it ran into Asia and Africa at times. It is fully described in Revelation, which was written 1700 years before the performance took place. When Napoleon had accomplished the things for which he was born his power suddenly left him and his enemies seized him and put him out on an island to die there alone. He came to his end and no one helped him, just as the prophecy of Daniel declared that he would; although the prophecy was written 2300 years before Napoleon was born. It described his character and what he would do and how he would come to his end suddenly. In reading it over, remember that Napoleon cared nothing for God in any way. He relied entirely on powder and muskets and handled them to his own notion. Brute force was *his* god.

> And the king (Napoleon) shall do according to his will; and he shall exalt himself and magnify himself above every god, and shall speak marvelous things against the God of gods; and shall *prosper* till the indignation be accomplished. Neither shall he regard the God of his fathers, nor regard any god, for he shall magnify himself above all. But he shall honor the god of forces (his armies). Thus shall he do in the most strong holds, with a strange god, which he shall acknowledge and increase. (Increase his armies.) And he shall cause them to rule over many, and shall divide the land for gain.—Daniel 11.

Napoleon subdivided kingdoms or threw them together into one—just as suited his purpose best; and he would put a relative or a friend in charge of some new subdivision which he had created.

> At the time of the end, shall the king of the south push at him (push at Napoleon); and the king of the north shall come against him like a whirlwind and he (Napoleon) shall enter into the countries and shall overflow and pass over.—Daniel 11.

Egypt (south of him) came at him, and then the countries north of him made a rush towards him, but he entered into those countries and overflowed or passed over them.

> He (Napoleon) shall enter also into the glorious land (Palestine) and many countries shall be overthrown. He

shall stretch forth his hand upon the countries and Egypt shall not escape. He shall have power over the treasures of gold, silver and all precious things of Egypt. But tidings out of the east and north shall trouble him (Napoleon) and he shall go forth with great fury to destroy and utterly to make away with many.—Daniel 11:41 to 44.

While Napoleon was in Egypt taking possession of the treasury and its gold and precious things and doing as pleased him best, the countries around his own home (France) rushed in to devour his headquarters (at home); and this was the "tidings out of the north and the east that troubled him," as set forth in the above prophecy; and he hurried back and *slashed* them and "utterly made away with many," as the prophet said he would.

He (Napoleon) shall come to his end and none shall help him.—Daniel 11:45.

And he *did* come to his end *suddenly*, and his enemies rushed in and seized him and took him to a lonely island, where no one could reach him to help him, just as the prophecy declared. How marvelous is God and His words! He showed to Daniel all the terrible and dreadful things which the beast with seven heads would do, and also pointed out how Napoleon would step onto the earth and halter the beast and stab it and let it bleed to death gradually. All this was shown to Daniel, mind you, 2300 years before Napoleon was born. Men have wondered and written about Napoleon the last 100 years. They have said all kinds of mean things about him and called him all manner of bad names, and have wondered why he was so successful in riding over the nations in the most desperate manner. It never occurred to the minds of historians that all his exploits and destiny were written out by God's inspired servants, thousands of years before they took place; and that Napoleon was simply following the record laid out for him, although he *never even suspicioned* that such was the case, as "he regarded not the God of his fathers (Abraham, Isaac and Jacob) nor any other god." He regarded the "god of forces" (armies and war), just as the prophet had declared. That hall in the Pyramid turned where I have it marked 324, and the world had to turn with it; and Martin Luther and others, working on the religious line, beating the beast with seven heads over the eyes; and Napoleon coming on afterwards and stabbing it with swords and turning the kingdoms around stopped the beast from running the world further down, as shown by the turn in the hall, where it ceased to slant and started on a level (horizontally). (See the hall at 324.) God was not only checking the beast (the pope and his church), but was pouring out upon it His indignation.

He (Napoleon) shall do according to his will and shall exalt himself and shall prosper *till the indignation* be accomplished.—Daniel 11:36.

This certainly answers the questions as to why Napoleon succeeded so astonishingly; and also why he came to his end suddenly, so that none could help him. Just so soon as the indignation on the beast (pope and Roman church) was accomplished, Napoleon came to his end. This should teach politicians and the public a sharp lesson about what causes this and that in governments; and why kingdoms go up or down, split or turn around. Politicians are always assigning some external cause for this, that and the other thing. As I write this chapter (1895), an ex-congressman, residing within a few miles from me, and well-informed he is on things political, is writing a book about Napoleon, and in it he is taking the position that Napoleon was a worthless man to the world, and that his success was caused by certain kinds of money in circulation in those countries at that time, and that when Napoleon introduced a different kind of monetary system it caused his defeat and brought his career to an end. I mention this one circumstance to show how badly deceived political people are about *causes* of success or failures in governments. Those who have no knowledge of spiritual things are always judging circumstances by *outside* appearances—never even dreaming that spiritual forces are constantly operating over us in our daily affairs. A man or a set of men will do a certain thing and all the world will rise up and strike at them, with the understanding that those men are the *cause* of the action. If we step in and proclaim it that the *real* cause is spiritual and that it lies behind the veil, unseen by the natural eye, we are laughed at as being fit subjects for the insane asylum. People *can not* or *will not* look behind the veil for the spiritual forces which run the world and turn governments, kingdoms and people up or down.

We wrestle not with flesh and blood, but with powers and principalities (spirits) in the air.—Ephesians 6:12.

The people are ignorant of this fact, and, as a consequence, they are constantly bumping their heads against stone walls and receiving deadly injuries; and they refuse to learn any thing on the godly line, and destruction continues to overtake them, physically, politically and spiritually.

> My people are destroyed for lack of knowledge; because they have rejected knowledge I will reject them. They have forgotten the law of God and I will forget their children. I will change their glory into shame. I will punish them for their ways. They shall eat and not have enough (famines and disaster strike them) because they will not take heed of the Lord.—Hosea 4.

The above scripture is forcing itself into action at this date, but politicians (ignorant of prophecy and spiritual things of course) think that it is the silver question, or the Democratic party, or the Populist party, or Republican party that is causing all this upheaval and unrest among the people. O, how tiresome and foolish their argument is to those who see behind the veil the forces at work to throw down and destroy the present governments of earth and establish a higher order of things. No political party can prevent this. Christ and the prophets and the apostles have declared that everything shall give way to the rule of Christ, and this is the *sole and only cause* for the present uproar and commotion among men.

> And in the days of these kings (governments) shall the God of heaven set up a kingdom, which shall never be destroyed, but it shall break in pieces and consume all these (present) kingdoms.—Daniel 2:44.
>
> And the seventh angel sounded, and there were great voices in heaven, saying, The kingdoms of this world are become the kingdom of our Lord and of his Christ.—Rev. 11:15.

And everything *now* is working to this destination. The people of earth are now dancing around the "pit" (the dark room under the Pyramid) each trying to push the other in. The struggle is *fierce*, as each person is determined to be head and grab the dollars, even if he must destroy his neighbors and friends to do it. The mad dance will commence in powerful earnest within eighteen years from 1896.

And the nations were angry and thy wrath is come.—Rev. 11:18.

The world has come down the long hall in the Pyramid, and the figures (in inches) indicate that this dispensation is now closing and the New Age is already taking root, to spread over the earth like a great tree.

The kingdom of heaven is like unto a grain of mustard seed planted in the ground, the least of all seeds, but when it is grown it is the greatest among herbs and becometh a tree, so that the birds of the air come and lodge in the branches thereof.—Matt. 13:31, 32.

The foundation is already set up and the seed is planted, the sprout is up and the buds are swelling and the great spiritual building is taking form *now on this earth*, and yet the general public does not notice it.

The kingdom of God cometh not with observation.—Luke 17:20.

The starting of it was represented to the prophet Daniel as a little stone cut out of a mountain without hands, and it grew until it covered the earth. See Daniel 2. It was the *starting* stone and it also became the top or cap-stone over everything else. Now notice how carefully this is represented in the Pyramid. As the Pyramid stands to-day it has no cap-stone. If the builders ever put it on it has been removed; but it is plausible to think that is was left off. It may be that it was hewn and brought onto the ground where the building was to be erected, and it served as a pattern for the whole structure. A Pyramid, having four sides and slanting inward, will, of course, come together in a sharp point at a certain distance from the base. The height of this point all depends on the slant. After a Pyramid is finished, the top or peak can be sawed off a few feet or many feet below and that top part, so cut off, still remains a perfect pyramid, only it is smaller. Its slant is the same as it was before being cut off, therefore, a mathematician can take that top part (so cut off) and by noting its slant, can figure out how many feet further down it would have to be extended so as to make a foundation a certain number of feet square; and after the foundation is laid, the small top peak, cut off, would show how much slant to give the sides in order to make them come together at the right height to meet the peak, so that it would set on and run to a peak on the same slant as it had been going. Thus nicely would this top-cap serve as a pattern for the whole work, from the ground up to the finishing point; and this being the case, the cap point would be made *first*, although it could not be put into the building until the very last, as it would not fit in at any other place on account of its peculiar shape; it would have five corners and five sides. The builders would, therefore, throw it aside as being of no value on account of its odd shape. It would be *rejected*. The workmen would consider it a nuisance on account of its always lying around in their way. They would *stumble* over it and swear at it and kick at it. It would be offending them by being in their way; but just wait until they run their building up to a height where the sides, on account of their slant, have come almost together at the top, so that a square stone or a flat stone or a round stone will not fit the place; then they will be at their wits' end to know what to do; finally, after trying to hunt out a stone that will fit, one of the workmen will pick up that five-cornered, peaked stone that had been so often cursed, kicked and stumbled over, and, in a half-angry, half-laughable manner, pitch it over to the other workmen and tell them to try *it* on the top of the building. Ah! It just fits the place. The slant is right, the five corners are right and the sharp peak is right. How nicely it completes the building. Hurrah for the rejected stone! It has become the very head of the building—the top stone over all. It occupies the highest seat. It gives beauty and form to the building. It splits the lightnings and throws them off as they dart down to destroy the great structure. It catches the first light descending from the heavens and divides it to all the sides. It kisses the clouds as they pass, and is in constant communication with the angels. Its high seat puts the world beneath it. All eyes are directed to it as it is the head corner. Its high position puts it into the pure atmosphere of God, while the lower (foundation) stones, which were *first* chosen, are served last; thus the *first* have become *last* and the last one becoms first. The whole order of things is reversed. Just so it will be again with the inhabitants of this earth in the near future. The preparations are being made for it now. The commotion is becoming greater and greater each year. Society and governments are becoming obnoxious and disgusting in the extreme, and will finally fall to pieces. Churches can no longer hold the confidence of the people as they used to do when the world was more ignorant than it is now. The morning light of the New Age is peeping up over the hills and dispelling the darkness caused by the seven-headed beast, and the people are catching glimpses of the *perfect* path from which the world has wandered, and they are gradually turning their backs on the old and dark order of things. Those who have been giving themselves over *entirely* to spiritual things and learning the ways and the will of God, and have been cursed, kicked and *rejected* by the world on account of it, are beginning to be elevated towards the top of the building, where they can be associated with the cap-stone in reigning over the earth. All eyes will be turned towards them, as they will judge the world; and in them will be deliverance or help to hand out to those who, in days past, rejected and arrested them.

And it shall come to pass that whosoever shall call on the name of the Lord shall be delivered: for in Mount Zion shall be deliverance, *and in the remnant whom the Lord shall call.*—Joel 2:32.

They shall be priests of God and of Christ and shall reign with him a thousand years.—Rev. 20:6.

The tabernacle of God is with men, and He will dwell with them, and they shall be His people, and God himself shall be with them. I make all things new.—Rev. 21:3-5.

The last (those rejected ones) will come first and the first ones last. Those who are piling up great heaps of property and grabbing after every material or worldly thing, and those who are striving for high political or social positions among men are now looked upon by the world as leaders. They must be *first* at everything. They get the *first* invitations to the banquets and are given seats at the head of the table. They lead the ball and dance next to the music. There is scarcely any deviltry going on over the earth without their presence to *lead* it. Their names always appear first at the top of newspaper

columns. "Hon. Soso and Her Royal Highness Soso
were present." While all these degrading things
are going on everywhere the *rejected* ones (called religious
cranks) are at home in their cabins meditating
in the deep silence to get the will of God in every
little daily transaction. They are seeking the voice
of the King to guide them, and when that Voice
speaks then the kingdom of God is in earth (fleshly
bodies) and God's will is being done in earth (in flesh)
as it is done in heaven. The King is then in command.
The Cap-Stone has been put on that person
and all his steps are guided by *It* and his wisdom
flows from It and he is a part of It and It is a part
of him. It is the head of him. He is in God and
God is in him. "He that hath seen Me hath seen the
Father." "The mystery that hath been hidden since
the foundation of the world but now revealed, viz.,
Christ *in* you."—Colossians 1:26, 27. And these people
who have gone back into the caves and cabins and
have cut loose from the world to commune with the
silence of God will, ere long, become *first* with the
head Cap-Stone and rule the world; while the "Hon."
and "Her Royal Highness" and "Judge" and "Gov."
and "Senator," etc., etc., will be *last* and not sit at the
head of the table. "Behold I make all things new."
—Rev. 21:5. These people who are to be associated
with the head Cap-Stone are now beginning to gradually
come together here in the United States of America.
It is merely the mustard seed yet, but time will
bring out its branches to cover the earth. In his vision,
Daniel saw the starting of it as a little stone
which grew until it covered the earth and broke up
all other kingdoms. Those who are coming together
to form the body of Christ (composed of many parts)

are not seen at any of the present church services, as each person has the "church" within him, and, therefore, needs no outside house in which to worship, as the worship goes on within himself. The revelation of God in the flesh is the rock on which Christ's church is built. The congregation, the house and the *Preacher* are all bound up within yourself. Your real spiritual self is the congregation to sit and listen. The Holy Ghost is the Preacher to instruct you, and your fleshly body is the temple in which the church services are carried on; therefore, you always have the house, the *Preacher* and the congregation with you.

The kingdom of God cometh not with observation. Neither is it over there or over here, for the kingdom of God is within you.—Luke 17:21. The mystery that hath been hidden from generations but now revealed, viz.: Christ in you.—Col. 1:26, 27. I am with you always, even unto the end of the world.—Matt. 28:20. Know ye not that your body is the temple of God.—1 Cor. 6:19. On this Rock (God in the flesh) I will build *My* Church and the gates of hell shall not prevail against it.—Matt. 16:18.

This solid church is now being brought together and carefully laid up, piece by piece, and it is composed of those who have discarded and cut loose from all the present church organizations and all preachers except the one great Preacher (Holy Ghost within), who teaches the same doctrine at all times and to all persons—leaving no open or doubtful places for the gates of hell to run in and pry open the building and divide it, as is the case with the church organizations of earth, who have Tom, Dick and Harry as preachers, who are simply feeding the people with intellectual *opinions*, so that there are almost as many *opinions* and different denominations as there are preachers. Their building has been dashed to many pieces and is sinking beneath the waves of unbelief and formality—caused by not having the Teacher (Holy Ghost). They cut themselves out of this Teacher by saying that "the day of miracles is past and that no man can communicate with God *nowadays.*"

The present great building that is being laid up is the Tabernacle of God shown to St. John in his vision.

> And I heard a great voice out of heaven saying, Behold, the tabernacle of God is with men and He will dwell with them and be their God (teacher).—Rev. 21:3.

It is the same structure as referred to by Isaiah and by Jesus as the *Elect.*

Having the Holy Ghost as their Teacher, of course they cannot be deceived by anybody or anything that may arise on earth. Deceptions and miraculous things are already starting up, but these people cannot be touched by any of them, as they are not depending on Bishop So-and-so and Reverend So-and-so to tell them which are genuine works of God.

> Ye are a *chosen* generation, a royal priesthood, a holy nation, a *peculiar people*, that ye should shew forth the praises of Him, who hath called you out of darkness into His marvellous light.—1 Peter 2:9.

When they are all gathered (as they will be within the next few years) they will be the grandest *spiritual* building on this earth. The great Pyramid was laid up with limestone and granite, but this present spiritual building is composed of live bodies.

> Ye also, as lively stones, are built up a spiritual house, a holy priesthood, to offer up sacrifices.—1 Peter 2:5.

And the finishing touch to this great spiritual building is the Cap-Stone (Christ) which forms the head or chief corner, but which the world rejected, just as the little five-cornered stone was rejected in the Pyramid on account of its odd shape. It was a "rock of offense," but, finally, became the chief stone and sat over all others.

Behold I lay in Sion a chief corner stone, elect, precious. The stone which the builders disallowed is made the head of the corner. A stone of stumbling and a rock of offense. A living Stone, disallowed by men but chosen of God.—1 Peter 2.

All through the Bible, Christ is represented as a stone, corner-stone, stumbling stone, rock of offense, etc. And the Millennial Kingdom of Christ is represented as a stone cut out without hands.

Thus saith the Lord, I lay in Zion for a foundation, a stone, a tried stone, a precious corner stone.—Isa. 28:16.

He shall bring forth the headstone with shoutings.—Zech. 4:7.

Those who are to compose the great spiritual temple, now being erected, are waiting in the Ante-Chamber, as represented in the Pyramid. They are being taught the ways of God, and when their spiritual education becomes completed they will be led into the King's Chamber or the *Most Holy* place, as represented in the Mosaic Tabernacle, where a special room was set apart for the Ark of the Covenant and none but the High Priest was allowed to approach it. That is, a person must be spiritually clean in order to enter into the room and dwell with God and have the Cap-Stone (Christ) put on him, *in* him and through him so that he can say "I am in the Christ and the Christ is in me. The kingdom of God is *within* me." The world has now come to the point when this Chief or Cap-Stone is to be set on. The rounding-out process of all past ages is now beginning with great force and velocity.

He will finish the work and cut it short in righteousness. A short work will the Lord make upon the earth.—Rom. 9:28.

Therefore, it is useless for political parties and churches to try to prop up the present order of things. *It can not be done.* The hour is come and the heavenly clock is striking, and every thing is in upheaval and will grow worse and worse until the entire political, religious and social system is completely ground into pieces and obliterated. Universal righteousness must and *will* take the place of the present ungodly state of things, but the greatest trouble and suffering the world has ever seen will precede the change.

THE HOARY PAST DUG UP.

Not many people know that the embalmed body of Pharaoh has been found, as the newspapers are so busily engaged in reporting murders and arguing politics that scarcely any of them even noticed this great "find."

RAMESES II. (PHARAOH).

The Hoary Past Dug Up. 131

After the body was found and unwrapped the genius of the Anglo-Saxon race showed itself when they sat Pharaoh up and took his photograph, and I now place it before you that you can look upon the features of the man who ruled over the Twelve Tribes of Israel (of whom we are a part) 3,300 years ago, when they were living near the mysterious Pyramid in Egypt. Little did he think then that we would hunt him up and dig him out. His nose, in the picture, is not in a natural condition, as the cloths and sheets wrapped around his head and face so tightly in the embalming process bent and flattened his nose down out of its natural position.

The Account of the Finding.

"Among the many discoveries recently made in Egypt, none have been of more interest than the finding of the mummified body of one of Egypt's kings, known in classic history as Rameses the Great, or Sesostris, and to Bible readers as the Pharaoh who oppressed the children of Israel. He was the foster-brother of Moses, and they doubtless grew up together as friends and companions until Moses cast his lot with the despised slaves, the sons of Jacob. Refusing to be called the son of Pharaoh's daughter, he chose rather to suffer affliction with the people of God than to enjoy sin for a season. Rameses became one of the mightiest rulers that Egypt ever knew. Under his reign the Israelites were greatly oppressed and their cries came up before God. Thirty centuries ago he died and his body was embalmed. It was found in an out-of-the-way place, and recently the bandages were taken from the body and the face that Moses looked upon three thousand years ago was seen to be in a good state of preservation. The body is now in the Egyptian Museum.

The following account is from the official report of Professor Gaston Maspero, director of the excavations and antiquities, who unrolled the body:

"The mummy (No. 5,233) first taken out from its glass case is that of Rameses II., Sesostris, as testified by the official entries bearing date the sixth and sixteenth years of the reign of the high priest Her-hor Se-Amen, and the high priest Pinotem I., written in black ink upon the lid of the wooden mummy-case, and the further entry of the sixteenth year of the high priest Pinotem I., written upon the outer winding sheet of the mummy, over the region of the breast. The presence of this description having been verified by His Highness the Khedive, and by the illustrious personages there assembled, the first wrapping was removed, and there were successively discovered a band of stuff, (sic) twenty centimetres in width, rolled round the body; then a second winding-sheet, sewn up and kept in place by narrow bands placed at some distance apart; then two thicknesses of small bandages; and then a piece of fine linen reaching from the head to the feet. A figure representing the Goddess Nut, one metre in length, is drawn upon this piece of linen, in red and white as prescribed by the ritual. The profile of the goddess is unmistakably designed after the pure and delicate profile of Seti I., as he is known to us in the bas-relief sculptures of Thebes and Abydos. Under this amulet there was found another bandage; then a layer of pieces of linen folded in squares and spotted with bituminous matter used by the embalmers. This last covering removed, Rameses II. appeared.

"The head is long, and small in proportion to the body. The top of the skull is quite bare. On the temples there are a few sparse hairs, but at the poll the hair is quite thick, forming smooth, straight locks about five centimetres in length. White at the time of death, they have been dyed a light yellow by the spices used in embalmment. The forehead is long and narrow; the brow-ridge prominent; the eyebrows are thick and white; the eyes are small and close together; the nose is long, thin, hooked like the noses of the Bourbons, and slightly crushed at the tip by the pressure of the bandages. The temples are sunken; the cheek-bones very prominent; the ears round, standing far out from the head and pierced like those of a woman for the wearing of earrings. The jawbone is massive and strong; the chin very prominent; the mouth small but thick-lipped, and full of some kind of black paste. This paste being partly cut away with the scissors, disclosed some much-worn and very brittle teeth, which, moreover, are white and well preserved. The mustache and beard are thin. They seem to have been kept shaven during life, but were probably allowed to grow during the king's last illness; or they may have grown after death. The hairs are white, like those of the head and eyebrows, but are harsh and bristly, and from two to three millimetres in length. The skin is of earthy brown, splotched with black.

"Finally, it may be said that the face of the mummy gives a fair idea of the face of the living king. The expression is unintellectual, perhaps slightly animal; but even under the somewhat grotesque disguise of mummification, there is plainly to be seen an air of sovereign majesty, of resolve and of pride. The rest of the body is as well preserved as the head; but in consequence of the reduction of the tissues its external aspect is less life-like. The neck is no thicker than the vertebral column. The chest is broad; the shoulders are square; the arms are crossed upon the breast; the hands are small and dyed with henna; and the wound in the left side, through which the embalmers extracted the viscera, is large and open. The legs and thighs are fleshless; the feet are long, slender, somewhat flat-soled, and dyed, like the hands, with henna. The corpse is that of an old man, but of a vigorous and robust old man. We know, indeed, that Rameses II. reigned for sixty-seven years, and that he must have been nearly one hundred years old when he died."

The discovery took place on the 5th day of July, 1881, and came about in this way: At Cairo, Egypt, a museum was established in which were placed all the curiosities discovered relating to the early history of the historic lands of the Pharaohs. The director of the museum, M. Maspero, observed for some time that travelers returning from Thebes brought with them relics of undoubted antiquity. Funeral offerings, pieces of papyrus and specimens of the sacred beetle of the ancient Egyptians, bearing the seals of Rameses II., and of Seti I., his father, were shown.

The director of the museum at once conjectured that an ancient tomb had been discovered by the Arabs, which they were stealthily robbing and disposing of their treasures to travelers as they found opportunity. The sequel showed that these conjectures were correct. By offering a large sum of money to an Arab guide he was induced to reveal the location of the underground tomb.

In the meantime M. Maspero had left Cairo, but his able assistant, Emil Brugsch, took up the work. On the 5th of July he was led by the wily Arab to the concealed entrance to the tomb, and so well was it concealed that one might pass and repass over it twenty times without ever suspecting it.

The entrance to the tomb was a shaft cut into the limestone rock, 40 feet deep and about 6 feet square. The shaft was filled with loose stones and the surrounding rock was also covered over with the same material so that to an observer it had the appearance of a ledge of loose stone. The stones taken out of the shaft, a passage was found to lead from the bottom of it to the heart of the mountain, a distance of about 250 feet. This terminated in a chamber, 13x23 feet in extent, and about 6 feet high. In this chamber was found the mummy of Rameses II., with the mummies of thirty-five others of the kings, queens and high priests of Egypt.

"Their gold coverings and their polished surfaces so plainly reflected my own excited visage that it seemed as though I was looking into the face of my own ancestors. The gilt face on the coffin of the amiable Queen Nofretari seemed to smile upon me like an old acquaintance. I took in the situation quickly with a gasp, and hurried to the air, lest I should be overcome and the glorious prize still unrevealed be lost to science.

"It was almost sunset then. * * * * The valley was as still as death. Nearly the whole of the night was occupied in hiring men to help remove the precious relics from their hiding-place. There was but little sleep in Luxor that night. Early the next morning three hundred Arabs were employed under my direction—each one a thief. One by one the coffins were hoisted to the surface, were securely sewed up in sail-cloth and netting, and then were carried across the plain of Thebes to the steamers awaiting them at Luxor."

The mummies were carried to Cairo and placed in the museum, where they may now be seen; and so, in God's own good time, the last resting-place of the oppressor of His people Israel was found. The mummy of this Pharaoh only adds another evidence to the truth of the Bible narrative. We read in Ex. 1:11, "And they built for Pharaoh treasure cities, Pithom and Raamses." Only last year the Egyptian Exploration Society discovered the ruins of the city of Pithom. The bricks of which it was built, 3,300 years ago, bear the seal and the name of Rameses II. Monuments that have been buried out of the sight of man these long ages attest to the fact that the city was built by Rameses II. The fact that Rameses II. built Pithom, taken in connection with the Bible account, shows that he was the Pharaoh who oppressed the sons of Jacob and afflicted them with burdens. This forever silences those Bible critics who have held that the story of Joseph and the sojourn of the Jews in Egypt was but a myth. Welhausen, one of the most learned of this school of critics, says, in view of the testimony of recent discoveries, there can be no doubt of the truth of the Bible narrative. Is not the hand of God visible in this work? And is he not now leading men to uncover the buried monuments of the past to put to shame this age of skepticism and infidelity?—*Messenger*.

The following comments are from Fowler and Wells' *Phrenological Journal*, New York.

The other mummy, that of Seti I., the father of Rameses, shows, if anything, a more kindly type of organization, the forehead being higher, broader, and the features softer in outline. He was "the new king

SETI I. (THE OLDER PHARAOH).

who knew not Joseph," as recorded in Exodus 1:8. He belonged to a new dynasty, wholly unconnected with that under which Joseph had attained to high office. It was he who built, to protect his frontier, the great wall and huge arsenals called in Exodus "treasure or store cities" (Ex. 1:11). As he grew older he associated with himself on the throne his son Rameses, then a boy of twelve years of age, who reigned jointly with him for about twenty years. When Seti died, Rameses reigned alone for forty-seven years, so that in all his reign covered a period of sixty-seven years. He was the Pharaoh whose daughter adopted Moses, and who ordered the murder of the children (Ex. 1:15-22).

It is a startling revelation of the hoary past that is presented us in these human relics of an Egyptian period, fully three thousand years ago—relics so well preserved that we can gather correct data of the appearance, age and physical characteristics of them when living. The new testimony they furnish of the truth of certain historical statements that have been much disputed is most valuable.—*Phrenological Journal.*

This is hard evidence against the teaching of our spiritualizing friends who hold that the Bible sayings are all spiritual and figures of speech, and that the *real* things never existed, but that the Bible writers simply fixed up some *allegories* to represent *principles.* How rapidly these critics are falling before the whizzing sickle of God. The people do not realize the intense darkness under which they are laboring concerning Bible teaching. How desperately true the words of St. Paul are when he says:

Blindness in part is happened to Israel until the fulness of the Gentiles be come in.—Rom. 11:25.

THE SECRET BRAND.

Obverse Side.   Reverse Side.

THE GREAT SEAL OF THE UNITED STATES.

The design was suggested by an Englishman, and was adopted by the Continental Congress of the U. S. June 20, 1782. The law provided for two sides to the seal—one to be called the *obverse* and the other the *reverse* side. The *obverse* (eagle side) is the one used on all public documents. The pyramid side is the tell-tale ear-mark slipped onto us to brand us as the Lost Tribes of Israel, who formerly lived in Egypt (Northern Africa) where the great mysterious Pyramid stands with its halls and slants and speechless record *supposed* to be the history of the Ages and God's plan of the different dispensations and turns of the human family. How wonderful is God!

Mankind has no idea of the marvelous working of an Unseen Force that is constantly shaping the destiny of nations and working out the path of individuals. Sometimes a small and unnoticeable thing on earth has wrapped up within it volumes and volumes of the history of the past, with a dial-plate marked and the hand set pointing to an *aston-*

ishing future. It walks in on time and sits down unnoticed and keeps its veil on until its time comes to speak, then it removes its covering and opens its mouth and rolls out a message from the eternal God that stuns the world. Its rumblings shake the earth and the inhabitants stand speechless. It is the voice of the Most High speaking to His creatures, and if our ears are trained to the heavenly music of the spheres we can trace the melody of the angelic host and beat time as they sing. Lift up your heads, ye nations, and look at the Lord your King. He is not dead, but liveth.

He marks your path and ye walk therein, whether ye know it or not. Ye are branded and kept in separate pastures according to His purposes. Thousands of years ago this great country of the United States of North America was laid off and destined for a purpose, but He covered His tracks behind Him so that no one could know the direction from which He came until He was ready for it to *be* known.

In my No. 2 book, called *The Millennial Kingdom*, and in No. 3, called *Our Near Future*, I have shown the movements of various nations and how they have been handled for a purpose, and that we, the Lost Ten Tribes of Israel, are a specially selected nation who descended from Jacob and resided with him in Egypt, right under the very shadow of the great Pyramid, 1,500 years before Christ. That we were led out of Egypt (by Moses). That we finally landed in Palestine and formed the grandest and most powerful kingdom on earth. It fairly glittered with its golden Temple and fixtures. The Bible tells us that even the Queen of Sheba was dumfounded and had no spirit left in her (on account of astonishment) when she visited it and saw the brilliant king (Solomon) with his fine chariots and handsome surroundings. We were then united with the Jews, and our great thrift made us forget God and He drove us out of the country and destroyed our kingdom, and King Shalmaneser took us into captivity 721 B. C.

> God stirred up the spirit of the king of Assyria, and he carried Israel away to the River Gozan unto this day.—1 Chron. 5:26.

> The Lord was very angry with Israel and removed them out of His sight; there was *none* left but the tribe of *Judah* (Jews) *only*.—2 Kings 17:18.

We were taken over to Media on the coast of the Caspian Sea, and from there we came to England, and finally, to America, where we could worship God in our own way; and here we are with our old ear-mark (the Pyramid) cut into our national seal. That Pyramid, in the shadow of which our forefathers Abraham, Isaac and Jacob lived nearly 4,000 years ago. Secretly and without suspicion, God forced His chosen people to this country and then handed to them their mark which had followed them down the ages. No wonder He, 2,500 years ago, commanded this new and then unknown country to keep still and not let the people know that it was already created and lying here ready to receive His special people when the time would come for Him to bring them.

> Keep silent before Me, O islands.—Isaiah.

But now, having brought us here, the Lord has cut the bands and let the long-hidden secret roll out before us to show to us who we are and what we are to do in the future. We had lost our own identity and thought that there was no hope of ever reaching that high godly condition which the prophets once knew. We were as old dry bones that had lain out and bleached by the elements of time.

> The hand of the Lord was upon me and set me down in the midst of a valley which was full of bones. They were very many and very dry. Thus saith the Lord unto these bones: I will cause breath (spiritual power) to enter into you. And breath (power) came into them and they stood upon their feet, an exceeding great army. Then He said: These bones are the whole House of Israel. They said, Our bones are dried and our hope is lost. But thus saith the Lord: Ye shall *know* that I am the Lord and I will put my spirit in you.—Ezek. 37.

The above prophecy is a clear statement of that which is to come upon us in the near future; but as this subject is fully presented in my books Nos. 2 and 3, it will not be discussed here. I, therefore, turn to our first settlement here in America. Of course we organized a government and were looking around for some emblem to carve on our Great Seal of State. Something suggested the Pyramid of Egypt as a fit thing to be pictured on the Seal of this government; and the Congress of the United States, in 1782, adopted it then and there, and it has been our ear-mark ever since. This was long before the people of this country knew anything about the Pyramid. John Adams received the suggestion from an Englishman; but what put it into the Englishman's mind? Why should *he* be so interested in fixing up a nice and peculiar seal for *this* country? It is just as the prophet Jeremiah says: "*Ah Lord God! There is nothing too hard for Thee to do.*" How secret is His work! He handles it right before the eyes of men, but they notice it not. Just look at the picture of the Seal set forth in this book and study its meaning.

First is the Pyramid picture, which whispers to us that we hail from the land of the Pyramid (Egypt), where our forefathers Abraham, Isaac and Jacob dwelt. You remember that the prophets say that *"The Lord has set signs and wonders in Egypt, even to this day."* Isa. 19:19, 20, Jer. 32. The *real* "sign and wonder" is in Egypt *yet*, as stone, while we, His specially chosen nation, carry a picture of it with us on our Seal so that all the world can see our "sign." It even opens our own eyes that have been blinded so many centuries (2,600 years), during most of which time we have not known who we are nor the source from which we came; but this was all carefully recorded by the Unseen Hand so that when He became ready to break the news to us and let us know ourselves, He would have the mile-posts and the *"sign-"* boards in their proper places, so that we could trace our path backward.

> I will bring the blind by a way that they (we) knew not. I will lead them in paths that they have not known. I will make darkness light before them. This will I do unto them and not forsake them. Let them (us) give glory unto the Lord and declare His praise in the islands (America).— Isa. 42:12-17. Bring forth the blind people. Who among them can shew us former things (our ancient origin). Let them bring forth their witnesses (we are now doing it). Ye are my witnesses, saith the Lord; my servants whom I have chosen. I will do a new thing. It shall spring forth. I will make a way in the wilderness (uncover our path).— Isa. 43.

At the top of the Pyramid on our Seal is a triangle, within which is that eye of God which has so carefully watched us during all the 2,600 years that we have been sojourning since the Lord drove us away from Palestine. We lost track of ourselves, but that Eye did not. It is the head corner or cap-stone on the Pyramid, and is surrounded by a triangle—three-sided, meaning Faith, Hope, Charity—Body, Soul, Spirit. Over the eye are these words: "*Annuit Coeptis,*" which mean, "*He prospers our beginning.*" Below the Pyramid are these words: "*Novus Ordo Seclorum,*" which mean, "*New era in the ages.*" Ah, the secret is let out by those words, although they were chosen and adopted by Congress in 1782 A. D., when the Millennial Kingdom was never thought of or talked about. The long lost "dry bones" were to have *Life* (God) put in them and stand up, an exceedingly *great army*, the prophet said; and only a *few* yet are beginning to breathe that Life, and in the *near* future will *stand up*. The building is commenced and the "New Era In The Ages" will be here soon, as expressed in our national Seal. The eagle is our emblem to represent swiftness and highness. We soar high. We go swiftly. We look piercingly into things. The eagle builds its nest in and inhabits the high places. It is strong, proud and commanding. The prophets talk about it and use it in a figurative way.

He shall come up and fly as the eagle.—Jer. 49:22. Though thou exalt thyself as the eagle and set thy nest among the stars (high up), etc., etc.—Ob. 4.

Yes, we are the *eagle* nation. We sit on the high places and watch the world. We lead; they follow. We, the Ten Tribes of Israel, are the people to whom God gave the kingdom when He took it away from Judah (Jews) for rejecting the Christ.

The kingdom of God shall be taken from you (Jews) and given to a nation bringing forth the fruits thereof.—Matt. 21:43.

In the Millennial Kingdom we are to become the

governors over Judah (Jews) and rule the nations of earth with the word of the Lord.

In that day I will make the governors of Judah (Jews) like an hearth of fire among the wood and like a torch in a sheaf. They shall devour all the people round about.—Zech. 12:6.

United with the Jews, as we will be, it will be the most powerful kingdom ever established. All this comes to us by the favor of God.

The Lord will set thee on high above all nations of the earth and make thee the head and not the tail and thou shalt be above and not beneath.—Deut. 28:1, 10, 13. The Lord hath chosen thee to be a special people unto Himself, above all other people upon the face of the earth. Thou shalt be blessed above all.—Deut. 7:6-14.

Without going further on this line, it is enough to say that sometimes the most trifling thing (seemingly so) contains volumes of wisdom, and we should learn that nothing *"happens,"* as everything has a *cause* behind it that is pushing it and a *reason* for being here, whether we can decipher it or not; and it serves its purpose and then disappears and something else comes forward in its stead. Thus it goes on and on in an endless chain to perfection, which is God; and the time is now dawning when the world is being swept rapidly towards a higher state.

"We now see as through a glass darkly, but when that which is *perfect* is come, *then* we shall see face to face."

THE GOLDEN MYSTERY.

In this day when God is uncovering the works of His own hand and permitting men to look thereon, it may be that the click of the telegraph will flash over the earth the astounding news that the golden Ark of the Covenant has been found, and in it a bowl of the manna which the Lord rained down from the heavens for the Twelve Tribes of Israel to eat while on their forty years' journey from Egypt to Palestine; also Aaron's rod which budded and blossomed so miraculously. The Ark of the Covenant was the most astonishing piece of furniture that ever sat on this earth. It was the wonder of the world nearly 900 years—from about 1491 B. C. to 600 B. C., then it suddenly slipped away and dropped out of sight, leaving no tracks of its whereabouts. The Bible has much to say about it down to a certain date, then its lips are sealed in the silence of God, Who has the wonderful furniture hid away (probably) until the proper time comes for Him to produce His cause and put His witnesses on the stand and astonish a faithless world.

Persons not familiar with the Old Testament are liable to ask what the Ark of the Covenant was. It was a small box or chest—something like a carpenter's tool-chest.

While Moses was leading the Israelites from Egypt to Palestine, the Lord called him up on Mount Sinai (about 1491 B. C.) and pictured out various things which He desired Moses to make and carry along on the journey, and this Ark or chest was one

The Golden Mystery. 147

THE ARK OF THE COVENANT.

See Exodus 25:10-23.

of them. It was to be made of wood and then overlaid with pure gold, inside and outside, with handsome gold border or molding around on the outside. The lid or top was to be pure gold (no wood in it) and on each end of the lid was to be a gold image representing an angel. These two angels were to face to each other and have their wings spread out. This golden lid was called the Mercy Seat. (See Exodus 25.) God, in spirit form, hovered over the Mercy Seat and talked with Moses and gave him instructions as to the journey and about the rules which were to govern the Twelve Tribes during what is called the Mosaic Dispensation, which covered a period of nearly 1,500 years. Then Christ came and set it all aside and gave the world a new order of things entirely, called the Christian or Gospel Dispensation, and in which we still live; but it is now drawing to a close; after which the Millennial Kingdom will set in; and the measurements in the halls of the Pyramid of Egypt and other things go to show that this age will close and the new one commence *about* 1915. It will not vary many years either way from this, as God is already gathering His Elect or chosen body of people and teaching them His spiritual laws and ways as mentioned in Rev. 7:3, Jer. 3:14, Matt. 24:40, 41, Joel 2:32, Isaiah 65:22. And this is why the Ark of the Covenant is so interesting at this time, as it was a *symbol* held up before the eyes of men to give them an idea of the *real* spiritual Tabernacle, which is just now being built; and as I see this spiritual building going up now, I recognize in it every little thing that was pictured out in that box or chest 3,300 years ago. When a person comes to the point of understanding the great spiritual network which is now being constructed by the Lord, he is astonished at the wisdom of Jehovah in taking a few boards and gold and constructing a most powerful lesson to train the minds of men. Of course the whole Tabernacle, Altar, shew bread, lamp, curtains and other fixtures connected with this Ark cut a figure in the lesson also; but in this chapter I am confining my remarks mostly to the golden Ark, as there are hints in the Bible and in other ancient writings which lead to the idea that the Ark is hid away and will be found when certain events occur on this earth; and as these occurrences are drawing near, a thought seems to come whispering down the ages, *"Look out for the golden Ark of the Covenant."* I do not hold to the idea that it will possess the wonderful power it had during the Mosaic Dispensation, as it was only a *symbol*, and it served its purpose *then*, and its power is now being transferred to the spiritual building in process of construction, and about which the Ark was teaching men. If you are not informed on the subject you will ask, What wonderful power did it possess? It possessed the whole power of God and that means everything. None but the High Priest, who was carefully washed and anointed, would dare touch it. If any other persons touched it, it would kill them instantly (Numbers 4:15). Other persons were not even allowed to *look* upon it, lest they die; therefore, the High Priest had to carefully conceal it under a cloth cover before allowing the men who were to carry it to come in and get it (Numbers 4:20). It had two large rings fastened on one side and two on the opposite side, and two long smooth poles, covered with gold, were put through the rings (one pole on each side) and they projected past the ends of the Ark far enough to be used as handles; and whenever it had to be moved, the chosen men for that purpose would take hold of the ends of those poles and lay them on their shoulders and walk off with it—some at the front and others at the rear (Exodus 25:12, 15). This Ark and the golden table and the golden candlestick and the golden Altar and the brass Altar were not allowed to be carried on

THE TWELVE TRIBES OF ISRAEL MOVING.

wagons, but had to be carried on the shoulders of men (Numbers 7:9 and 3:31). All the other furniture of the Tabernacle could be transported on wagons, and it took six covered wagons and twelve oxen to draw them—two wagons for the heavy curtains and the other four wagons for the boards covered with gold and the brass pillars.

God stayed with this Ark (chest) and talked to Moses and gave him instructions (Numbers 7:89); and this is why unholy persons would not dare touch it or look upon it; the spiritual power of God would devour them. Even the High Priest had to wash himself carefully before going near it. This shows how very clean and pure a person must be mentally and spiritually before he can *touch* God. Think on this point and then look over the world and see how many persons, in the churches or out of them, are touching God or anywhere near Him.

This Ark was carried along with the Israelites during all that forty years, and a cloud hovered over it day and night; at night the cloud looked like a pillar of fire. The Israelites were to follow the cloud. When it stood still they camped. If it started off in the night they pulled up stakes and went along with it. At the end of their forty years the cloud took them up to the east bank of the Jordan River, which runs south through Palestine, and He told them that they must cross it in order to come into the land which He had set apart for them. He ordered the priests to take the golden Ark and go before and lead the way. The river was up high in the banks, as it usually overflows during all that season of the year (harvest time). So soon as the feet of the priests who were carrying the Ark touched the water it ceased flowing on down and stood still or backed up the stream, leaving the bed of the river dry. The priests with the Ark advanced to the center of the river bed and stood there while all the great army (about two million persons) passed over the dry land. After all had reached the opposite bank, the priests with the Ark marched out also (Joshua 4:7, 23). The priests then took the Ark and carried it around the city of Jericho, and the walls of the city fell down (Josh. 6).

The Israelites went to war with the Philistines, and Israel was defeated; they then took up the Ark and carried it out to where the next fight was to occur. They supposed that this Ark would cause them to defeat the Philistines, but the Lord had not commanded them to do such a thing and He let the battle go against Israel again and the Philistines captured the Ark and took it off with them (1 Samuel 4:1 to 12). A messenger came from the battlefield to notify the priest that the Ark had been captured. When the word *Ark* was spoken, the priest fell off his seat and broke his neck (1 Samuel 4:18). The Philistines took the Ark and set it in their house of worship, by the side of their big idol which they named *Dagon* and which they worshiped as *their* God; during the night Dagon fell down in front of the Ark. Next morning they set Dagon back to his place, but that night he fell down again and broke his head and hands off, in front of the Ark. Of course it was the Spirit of God in the Ark that was knocking the idol down, and the Philistines took a hint and became afraid of the Ark; diseases and trouble were striking the Philistines thick and fast. They moved the Ark away to another town, but so soon as it arrived destruction began in that town also, by a terrible disease striking the people. They moved the Ark to another town, but destruction set in there too. They called a council to decide what to do with the Ark, as they were afraid to dstroy it, lest the Lord might visit worse plagues upon them. They decided to put it on a wagon and then hitch two cows to the wagon and turn them loose and let them take it as they pleased. The idea was, that if the Lord wanted the Israelites to have possession of the Ark He would direct the cows toward the land of Israel. The cows had young calves; and to make

COWS DRAWING THE ARK OF THE COVENANT.

it still more *testing* as to whether the Lord was directing the cows, the calves were taken from them and kept with the Philistines. If the cows would turn away from their calves and go towards Israel it would show that God was influencing the cows.

The cows (hitched to the wagon) were turned loose, and away they went to the Israelite community. (See 1 Samuel 6.) The Israelite people saw the cows and the Ark come down the road and turn into a field of an Israel man and stop at the side of a big rock, and some harvest hands went and took the Ark down from the wagon and set it on the rock; and of course they were curious (just as people are now) to examine the Ark, and they lifted the lid and looked into it and it slew 50,070 persons in the neighborhood for looking in. The Lord had given everybody warning to stay away from it, but they disregarded the warning (1 Samuel 6:19).

I pause to relate a remarkable circumstance about the road over which the cows traveled when drawing the Ark from the Philistines to the Israel people. Palestine is rough, with (in some places) only narrow valleys or ravines winding around between the hills. The roads, of course, followed these valleys. The railroad recently constructed from Joppa to Jerusalem follows the same valley or road over which the cows traveled in going towards Jerusalem, 1,100 years before Jesus of Nazareth was born. As one rides along on the train to-day the valley of Beth-shemesh, into which the cows came with the Ark, is in plain view at the side of the railroad.

> And they of Beth-shemesh were reaping their wheat harvest, in the valley: and they lifted up their eyes and saw the Ark and rejoiced to see it. And the cart came into the field and stood there where there was a great stone.—1 Samuel 6:13, 14.

Little did the harvest hands then in the valley think that a swift whirling train of cars, drawn by locomotives manufactured in a great unknown country called America, would, 3,000 years later, come steaming down that same road and whirl past them on its way to Jerusalem. Ah, God, Thou art marvelous!

The Israel people then removed the Ark to a man's house, where it remained twenty years (1 Samuel 7:1, 2). David became king over Israel and he sent to that house for the Ark. They put it onto a wagon and started with it, but on the road the oxen either stumbled or in some way shook it, and one of the men put out his hand and touched it to steady it and he fell over dead instantly. This displeased David and also made him afraid to remove it further, so he had it placed in another man's house, where it remained three months and caused that man to prosper abundantly (2 Samuel 6:11); then David sent for it again, but this time he ordered it carried on the *shoulders* of men (as the Lord had instructed Moses) and it came through all right, and David placed it in a tent which he made for it (2 Samuel 6). After David died, Solomon became king and built the great Temple and removed the Ark into it about 1005 B. C. (1 Kings 8:1 to 12). Whenever any of the Israelites fell into trouble, if they would turn their faces towards the Temple, wherein was the Ark, the Lord would send relief.

The Ark remained there until about 606 B. C., since which time no human being can trace its whereabouts. About that date (606 B. C.), Nebuchadnezzar, king of Babylon, came over with an army and destroyed the Temple and took the people captive. He carried away all the gold and fixtures about the Temple, but he did not get the Ark, as a list of articles which he took is set out in the 52d chapter of Jeremiah, but the Ark is not in the list; and if it had been in the Temple he would have picked on it *first*, as it was gold and very vauable in many ways.

Josephus, the Jewish historian, who lived about the time of Christ, speaks in his writings about the king of Babylon destroying the Temple and carrying the furniture away; and he gives a list of it, but the Ark is not in his list. It is a certain thing that the Ark had been taken out of the Temple before the siege struck the city, and as Jeremiah was the servant of God at that date he was foreshown that the army from Babylon would come over to Jerusalem and destroy the Temple; and it is quite reasonable to think that Jeremiah took the Ark out of the Temple and hid it away to prevent the army from getting it. There are some hints of this kind in the various ancient writings. In the old Bibles which were in use fifty years ago were a lot of writings called Apocrypha, and which were always considered as not being inspired, and for this reason the Bibles of to-day do not contain those writings; but even if they were not inspired they contained much history on valuable points, among which I find the following in 2 Maccabees 2:4, 8:

"It was also contained in the same writing, that the prophet, being warned of God, commanded the Tabernacle and the Ark to go with him, as he went forth into the mountain where Moses climbed up and saw the heritage of God; and when Jeremy came thither, he found a hollow cave, wherein he laid the Tabernacle and the Ark, and the Altar of Incense, and so stopped the door. And some of those that followed him came to mark the way, but they could not find it, which, when Jeremy perceived, he blamed them, saying, 'As for that place, it shall be unknown until the time that God gathers His people again together and receives them in mercy. Then shall the Lord show them these things; and the glory of the Lord shall appear, and the cloud also, as it was shown unto Moses.' "

The above is rather stunning evidence that the Ark is to be found when God gathers His people together again; and as He is now gathering His Elect it is not unreasonable to think that this great and wonderful Ark will roll out before the eyes of the people ere long. Some think that Jeremiah took it to Ireland about 585 B. C., and that a king built a tomb for his dead wife and put the Ark in it and then covered the tomb over with a great mound of earth and called the mound *Tara*, which means two tables. The Ark contained the two stone tables on which were written the Ten Commandments given to Moses; and as *Tara* means two tables, it is a suspicious circumstance that forms a link in the chain of evidence about the Ark. Very old history of Ireland seems to hint something about Jeremiah coming there, but of course the Lord has been very careful not to allow any definite history made about the Ark if it is His intention to spring it upon us as a stunning witness; and many things go to show that such is His aim. He told Moses to save a potful of the manna as a witness for generations, that they might see the kind of bread which the Lord furnished to the Israelites during their forty years' journey. Moses told Aaron to attend to it, and Aaron laid it up before the Testimony (Exodus 16:32-35). The two stone tables of Testimony were kept in the Ark; and 1 Kings 8:9 says that nothing else but those were in it when Solomon placed it in the Temple, but St. Paul, in Hebrews 9:4, says that the golden pot of manna and Aaron's rod that budded were also in the Ark. The word *"wherein"* in verse 4 may mean the *room* in which the Ark sat.

If the articles mentioned in Hebrews were ever in it they must have been taken out. The Ark was for some time in the possession of the Philistines after the death of Eli, and was opened (see 1 Samuel 6:19), so they may have been removed then. It is, however, more probable that the word "wherein," in Hebrews, refers to the room in which the Ark was kept. There was a coffer there with the Ark, containing other precious things (see 1 Samuel 6:15), in which the manna and the rod were likely to be kept. But however this may be, the Ark is certainly in existence, and circumstances go to show that it will be uncovered by the Lord at the proper time. A careful study of its history and its meaning and the meaning of all the fixtures in and about the Tabernacle is the most valuable lesson men can learn at this time. It will teach them what is soon to come on this earth in the New Age. It teaches the peculiar and important service to be performed by the *Elect* body of persons now being brought together to compose the Tabernacle of God, as mentioned in Rev. 21:3.

I heard a great voice out of heaven saying, Behold the Tabernacle of God is with men and God himself shall be with them.

God's power stayed with the golden Ark and would talk with Moses from that place and give instructions. When they carried the Ark to the Jordan River the water parted and let the Israelites pass over. When they carried it around the city of Jericho the walls fell down and let them enter in and take possession. Whenever any thing would go wrong with the Israelites all they had to do was to look towards the Temple, wherein the Ark sat, and pray to God there for help and help would come. God was centered there in that building. Just so it will be in this new spiritual building now being constructed. The tangible or outside part of it will be made up of human beings (lively stones, 1 Peter 2:5); but the power of God will be with them to deliver the world from its trouble.

<small>And it shall come to pass that whosoever shall call on the Lord shall be delivered, for in Zion shall be deliverance and in the *Remnant* whom the Lord shall call.—Joel 2:32.</small>

This Elect body of persons, composing the great Tabernacle, will be *as* God and shall not only have power of *deliverance*, but all other power, as was represented by the golden Ark and the Tabernacle, for the reason that Christ will be in these people and He doeth the works.

<small>In that day, the House of David shall be *as* God, as the angel of the Lord before the world.—Zech. 12:8.</small>

Having such wonderful power, of course they overcome death and walk right over it and trample it under foot and live on like a tree.

<small>There shall no more be an infant of days, for the *child* shall die an hundred years old; for as are the days of a tree shall the days of my people be, and mine *Elect* shall long enjoy the work of their own hands.—Isa. 65:20-22.</small>

It is easily seen that people with such power of God could not be deceived, as it would be like deceiving God—a thing impossible.

<small>There shall arise false Christs and false prophets and shall shew great signs and wonders, so that if it were possible they would deceive the very *Elect*.—Matt. 24:24.</small>

They will be a chosen body of persons to act as a Royal Priesthood, and, as such, must be fully *washed* before going in before the Lord, just as Aaron, the high priest, had to wash himself in *water* before touching the Ark. These coming priests will all be washed, *not* in water, but by the *Spirit.*

Ye are a chosen generation, a Royal Priesthood, a holy nation; as lively stones are ye built up a spiritual house, a holy priesthood.—1 Peter 2:5, 9.

They will be the same stature or height (spiritually) as Jesus was and will do the miracles He did and greater ones.

Till we *all* come in the unity of the faith, unto a *perfect* man, to the measure of the stature of Christ.—Eph. 4:13.

He that believeth on Me, the works that I do he shall do also; and greater works than these shall he do.—John 14:12.

By this it must *not* be understood that I deny the divinity of Christ. I simply take His own words as to how *great* men can and *will* become during the Millennial age, which is soon to set in, when "Thy will be done in earth as in heaven." This great spiritual company now being built together will be known to all the world and all nations will look to it for teaching about God, especially at the *beginning* of the New Age.

It shall yet come to pass that the inhabitants of many cities shall come, saying, Let us go speedily to seek the Lord; for in those days ten men shall take hold out of all languages of the nations, even shall take hold of the skirt of a Jew, saying, We will go with you, for we have heard that God is with you.—Zech. 8:20-23.

I will get them praise and fame in every land, even in the time that I gather you, for I will make you a name and a praise among all people of the earth, when I turn back your captivity before your eyes, saith the Lord.—Zephaniah 3:19, 20.

The *captivity* mentioned in the above scripture

is fully shown and explained in my Millennial Kingdom book, in which the dates and facts are presented. This coming spiritual nation (the Elect) are the same as foreshown in Rev. 7. The sealing mentioned there is now going on, and the extreme trouble and tribulation which are to stike the earth are being held back until the "sealing" of this Royal Body of High Priests is accomplished. (Notice Rev. 7:1-5.) They will take the place of Aaron, the high priest, who stayed close to the golden Ark; indeed they will be the Ark, the priest, the Tabernacle, the Altar and all the fixtures, and the power of deliverance will be in them as it was in the Ark. Failures of crops and tribulations will be swept from the world and general peace and godliness will take possession; but before this great change can come, a season of many years of afflictions, pestilences, failure of crops, floods, drouths, new diseases, insanity, wars and dreadful tribulation will set in. Indeed they are already here in mild form, but growing worse each year, so that men are complaining that there is no work for themselves or teams, and that they are sick physically, financially, and morally; and that every man is up and against his neighbor, trying to cheat him and beat him in every way, so that existence seems so burdensome that many are suiciding. This is all set out in the prophecies as having to come before the Millennial age, with its goodness, can set in; but people are not acquainted with the prophecies, and, therefore, can not discern what the matter is just now, and what causes such a dreadful stagnation in business affairs and trouble in every way. If they will read what God's prophets said about these times they will see something.

Before these days there was no hire for man nor beast; neither was there any peace on account of afflictions, for I set all men, every one against his neighbor; but *now* (in the New Age soon to set in) I will not be unto the remnant of this people as in the former days, for the seed shall be prosperous; the vine shall give its fruit and the ground shall give its increase, and the heavens shall give their dew; and I will cause the *remnant* of this people to possess all these things.—Zech. 8:10-12.

Ah, if the people could be made realize the *dreadful* scourging soon to fall upon this earth, it *seems* as though they would drop their extreme foolishness and turn over a new leaf; not through fear or selfish purpose, but because they owe better service to God and to themselves and their children. God has been lenient and merciful to the world, but mankind seems prone to run after every thing but the good. So long as they are prosperous and have plenty to eat and a bed in which to sleep and no pains to bother them they never think about God, man nor any thing; and the only way to make them think, it *seems*, is to heat the branding-iron red-hot and put it to them until it burns into the flesh and causes extreme agony; then they cry for help. This is exactly what they will do within a few years from now. The time is expiring. This age is about to close and the Millennial age is about to start in, and its grandeur and goodness is a great prize worthy to seek. Human intellect can not form an idea of the brilliancy and peacefulness of it. This is why the prophet Daniel says that it will be a great favor indeed to be born onto the earth at the *right time* to meet this new order of things.

Blessed is he that waiteth (birth held back) and cometh to the 1335 days.—Daniel 12:12.

As this branch of the subject is discussed in my books Nos. 2 and 3, it will not be dwelt upon here.

ANCIENT ASSYRIAN TABLETS FOUND.

The veil which has hung over the face of the earth 6,000 years or more and shut out from sight the tracks and turns in the path of the ancient inhabitants of earth is now being removed and we are permitted to look back on the hoary past, and, with breathless astonishment view the movements of nations and of individuals; and as we do so we find the key to the mysterious statements of the Bible writers who understood the situation and wrote accordingly; and it is only after we have a knowledge of the "lay of the land" and the circumstances surrounding it that we can read about a country and its history understandingly. *Then* the statements become live words so that our minds grasp the harmony of the narrative and makes it seem as of only yesterday. The world has passed through many struggles. Men have come onto the stage of action and played their part and turned the human family into new paths and then left the earth for new hands to manipulate. One common purpose is behind it all. That purpose is the perfection of mankind and redemption of all the earth. Sometimes the changes and weavings in the great plan have become stormy and turbulent so that the final outcome could not, just at the time, be discovered or understood, but the untiring Hand overturns and overturns until the corners are rounded and the great building of God takes on the required form so that its general outline can be seen through the scaffold-work. One of the men who helped to divide, destroy, build up, turn and change men and governments was Sennacherib, a king of Assyria, who was on the earth about 700 B. C. He came on as king of Assyria (the country away northeast of Palestine) soon after the Ten Tribes of Israel were taken captive and led over in that direction to the Caspian Sea, which is still east of the Assyrian country. In reading about this country (Assyria) you must be careful not to get the idea that it is Palestine, as such an idea will throw you into hopeless confusion so that the Bible narratives become a great tangled mess of contradictions, as the Bible has much to say about Assyria and Syria, which are two countries with widely different histories. Notice the difference in the spelling of the two names. Syria took in the northern part of Palestine and went east 150 miles to the Euphrates River and sometimes (under certain rulers) still further east to the Tigris River. Then, on the east line of Syria commenced Assyria, which was inhabited by the Gentiles who worshiped idols and carried on high carnival; while Syria west of Assyria was inhabited by a powerful Hittite kingdom and a mixture of other people, all Gentile idol-worshipers except the Israelites, who knew the true God, but they gradually fell into the ways of their neighbors and worshiped idols too, although they were under the Israelite government, which was almost continually in controversy with the Assyrian country east of Syria. The two countries (Syria and Assyria) were nearly always spiting each other, and the final wind-up of it all was that the Israelites were captured and taken away *by force*, and they have never returned. It is pretty clearly proven that we, the Anglo-Saxons (English-speaking people

of the United States and of England and a few
others) are those people who were captured by
the Assyrians. So here we are, away out here in
the United States of America, the leading nation of
the world, while our ancient homestead is now inhabited by the desperate and terrible Turks; and
the Assyrians who took us (721 B. C.) lost their
government and have been marauding around in
ups and downs 2,500 years. The Bible has much
to say about our ancient trouble with the Assyrians
and the record of it is plain after one understands
the "lay of the land" and the surroundings at *that*
time, and this is why I mention this man Sennacherib, the dashing king of Assyria, as he played
a bold part in our ancient homestead (Palestine).
He had a hankering to be looking after us (over in
Canaan) in a way that would be to the most advantage to him and his country of Assyria, which, as
I have mentioned, lay east of Palestine. He had
swept down several nations so successfully that he
had the idea that nothing could stand against him.
He came over to Palestine and bombarded the Jewish kingdom and forced the king to pay him money
and valuables. The Jewish king raked up all the
money he could find and paid it over and also cut
the gold off the Temple doors and from the pillars
and handed *that* over to the Assyrian king (2 Kings
18:13, 16). Some time after this plundering the
Assyrian king sent word that he would come again
and cut them down if they did not obey his dictates.
He sent word that the God of the Jews could not
prevent him from destroying the Jewish kingdom,
and in support of this argument he referred them to
the other nations who had trusted in their wooden

gods (idols) and failed. He thought the God of the Jews was like the gods of other nations, but herein he made a great mistake. The God of the Jews was the ruler of the universe, but Sennacherib did not believe it, so he came on with a great army to attack the Jews and camped just outside the city, and that night the angel of the Lord struck down 185,000 men of the Assyrian army. When morning came there lay the great number dead. Sennacherib came to the conclusion that it was a dangerous move to attack the God of the Jews and he, therefore, turned his steps homeward to Nineveh and worshiped his own idol god; and while he was in the *very act* of bowing to his idol two of his own sons slipped up behind him and killed him. (See 2 Kings 19:35-37.) This peculiar narrative in the Bible has always been regarded with suspicion as to the *truth* of it, but just recently some ancient Assyrian tablets have been dug up in Asia, and on one is printed a history of this identical tragedy, which agrees in every respect with the Bible account of it. The slab is of unbaked clay. It deals with the wars and assassination of this man Sennacherib as follows:

"On the 20th day of Tobit (modern December-January), Sennacherib, King of Assyria, in a revolt his sons killed him. On the 18th day of Adar (February-March), Esarhaddon, his son, sat on the throne of Assyria."

Now read the Bible statement about this same occurrence and see how closely it agrees with the ancient clay slab, dug up from its grave to beat an unbelieving world.

And it came to pass, as Sennacherib was worshipping in the house of Nisroch, his god, that Adrammelech and Sharezer his sons smote him with the sword; and they escaped into the land of Armenia. And Esarhaddon his son reigned in his stead.—2 Kings 19:36, 37.

His assassination occurred about 680 B. C. How nicely and quietly God has prepared things to come forth at the proper time to stop the mouths of a proud and stiff-necked people. Ah, but there will be a rattling of dry bones in the near future that will make the teeth of people clatter. They will hunt the holes in the rocks and crawl in, trembling, "when the Lord cometh out of his holy habitation to shake terribly the earth." They will not stop to argue Him out of existence as they *now* try to do.

The spiritual twisters and symbolizing critics have, no doubt, argued that no such a man as Sennacherib ever existed. All symbol. No sons ever killed him. He never marched against Jerusalem. Never lost 185,000 men all in one night by the hand of God. All symbol to represent a principle, they say. I presume that they will now say the clay tablet containing the history of his assassination never existed. All symbol, meaning some spiritual thing in the sky, and that the *real* tablet never existed *at all*. I often meet with people who are honestly trying to be Christians, and yet they have these curious ideas about all the Bible statements being figures of speech, and that the *real* things never occurred. Things are now coming to light that will overthrow all such abominable stuff. Thousands of clay tablets (slabs) are now being dug up out of the ruins of Nineveh, Babylon, Jerusalem, Egypt and elsewhere that have printed on them the important history of ancient times; and this clay slab history throws light on many of the Bible narratives. For instance: This man, Sennacherib, built for himself, in Nineveh, a fine palace, covering eight acres of ground, and having 60 rooms on the first floor and a hall 180 feet long and 40 feet wide. He went over to northern Palestine, hundreds of miles west of him, and cut down the cedars of Lebanon and drew them over to Nineveh and used them in his palace building. This is what the prophet Isaiah is hitting at in his writings about Sennacherib, who claimed that he could do as he chose, and that he intended to come against the Jewish kingdom at Jerusalem, and that the God of the Jews could not hinder him; but I have shown that He *did* hinder him most severely by striking down 185,000 of the Assyrian soldiers in one night. Sennacherib had been cutting and hauling the fine cedars out of God's chosen country (Palestine) and doing other bold exploits long enough, and the Jewish king laid the matter before the Lord and asked protection, and the Lord, through the prophet Isaiah, spoke as follows:

Then Isaiah said: Thus saith the God of Israel: Whereas thou (*the Jewish king*) hast prayed to me against Sennacherib, king of Assyria, this is the word which the Lord hath spoken concerning him: By thy servants hast thou (Sennacherib) reproached the Lord and said: By my chariots I come up to the sides of Lebanon (mountain) and I will cut down the tall cedars and choice fir trees thereof and will enter into the forests of Carmel. With the soles of my feet have I dried up all the rivers of the besieged cities. (*He had torn up the country and was boasting of it and how he intended to do so again.*) Therefore, thus saith the Lord concerning the king of Assyria (Sennacherib), He shall not come into this city (Jerusalem).—Isa. 37:21-38.

And he did not accomplish his second raid. He lost his men and had to turn back to his home where he had his fine palace, the interior of which was finished with carvings and paintings of generals of the army and horses, etc., drawn on the walls and painted a bright red (called vermilion).

The pictures were flashy and brilliant to look upon. War scenes and other exploits were "portrayed" on the walls of the great palace which was located in the city of Nineveh which, history says, was 21 miles long and 9 miles broad, which would make 60 miles around it. It is claimed that the wall around the city was 100 feet high and so broad that three carriages could drive, side by sde, on top of it. It had 1,500 towers, each 200 feet high, shooting up from the walls. The city was destroyed *about* 600 B. C., and its ruins were covered over by dirt and rubbish being blown upon it, so that it was buried as in a grave, just as the prophecies declared it *would* be. The covering of dirt over it was so complete that the ruins had the appearance of being natural hills, and people (hundreds of years afterward) regarded them as such until recently they have been dug up and the buried buildings brought to light. The ruins make a mound about 60 miles around it, which shows that the history declaring the size of the city to have been 60 miles in circumference is correct. The inhabitants were wicked and carried on with a "high hand" against the God of the Jews, as the Assyrians (Nineveh people) knew nothing about a *spiritual* God, as *they* had wooden and stone gods (idols) and trusted in them and laughed at the Jewish idea about an unseen God in spirit form; and they (the Ninevehites) would tantalize the Jews and sneer at the God of Israel, and run over into Palestine and sweep down the Jewish cities and then laugh at the weakness of the God of the Jews for not being able (as the Nineveh people thought) to protect them. The God of Israel permitted them to go on in this way for a time and then He told the prophet Jonah to go over to Nineveh and tell the people there that if they would not repent and behave themselves He would surely destroy the city. Jonah knew the people over there would laugh at him and sneer at his God, so Jonah tried to avoid the command of the Lord by starting out in the opposite direction and running away. He took the first ship going west and after they were away out on the water a storm came up and dashed the ship around like mad so that the officers and passengers put their heads together to know what they would better do, and they came to the conclusion that there was on the ship somebody who was causing the raging storm and that he must be put out in order to prevent the ship from sinking. They did not know which one of the passengers was the cause of the trouble, and so they agreed to cast lots on the matter and then stand by its decision. The lot fell on Jonah, and they gathered hold on him and threw him out into the water and a large fish swallowed him, and he remained in its belly three days and three nights and then the Lord caused the fish to vomit Jonah out on dry land, after which the Lord told him to go over to Nineveh and tell the people that message which He had delivered to him before he (Jonah) started to run away. Jonah's experience had taught him that it was useless to try to run away, therefore, he went to Nineveh and did as the Lord commanded, and the people repented (see Jonah 3); but it seems that they soon forgot it and fell back into their old ways, and the city was destroyed at last and covered over with dirt, just as the prophecies had declared.

> Woe to the bloody city. It is full of lies and robbery. I am against thee, saith the Lord. I will shew the nations thy nakedness and shame. I will cast abominable filth upon thee; and it shall come to pass that all who look upon thee shall flee and say, Nineveh is laid waste. The fire shall devour thee and the sword shall cut thee off and eat thee up. Thy nobles shall dwell in the dust.—Nahum 3.

The above prophecy came true with the rigidness of iron, and that once great city was ruined and buried and slept beneath the dirt which covered its shame so that during all of those 2500 years men passed by its location believing that the mound caused by its ruins was a natural hill until recently Layard, Botta, Smith and others have dug her out from her grave, and they find temples, palaces and buildings whose walls are decorated with paintings of armies and horsemen and other scenes, all painted in vermilion (a bright red color), which go to prove that the prophets had been there and looked upon those gay red pictures while the city was in its greatest prosperity; and of course the spirit of the Most High told the prophets that the gay and flourishing city would meet with a great calamity and that all of those pictures and images and carved walls should go under the dirt on account of the wickedness of its people. The prophet Ezekiel was captured and taken over there in that Assyrian country when the other Israelites were captured, and he (the prophet Ezekiel) gave his Israelitish brethren a good sound lecture on the reason why they were captured and held as prisoners over there by the Assyrians. He told the Israelites that the ungodly idol ways of the Nineveh people had attracted the eyes of the Israel people so greatly that they (the Israelites) had forgotten God. Those gay red pictures and the army of men mounted on prancing horses and parading through the streets of Nineveh were more flashy to look at than God (according to the Israelites' idea) and as a consequence God had permitted them to be captured and held there as prisoners. Now notice how plainly Ezekiel lays it down to them; and it shows that he had seen these identical palaces of Nineveh and had looked upon the carvings and red pictures on the walls which we are just now digging out from under the dirt and bringing them to the light so that all nations can look upon them and form a correct idea of what the city used to be 3,000 years ago. Now hear Ezekiel tell it; but before reading it I must explain to you that he was lecturing about the Ten Tribe kingdom of Israel which occupied the northern half of Palestine, and the Judah kingdom which occupied the southern half. You remember that I have shown to you in my books Nos. 2 and 3 how the Israelitish kingdom was divided into two parts on account of the quarrel they had among themselves. The northern kingdom (Ten Tribes) was called Israel or Samaria, while the southern kingdom was called Judah or Jerusalem. You must remember this and these names if you want to understand the prophecies, as they refer to them as Israel and Judah or Samaria and Jerusalem or Judea. Ezekiel, in his lecture, calls them two women, because they were always acting the harlot; that is, they were doing things against God, and he (Ezekiel) compares them to two sisters who had fallen in love with the Assyrians and the gay way over there. He was hitting at Israel and Judah for wanting to associate with those heathen

Assyrians who worshiped idols. Now you can understand Ezekiel's lecture.

> The word of the Lord came to me saying: There were two woman (Israel and Judah) and they committed whoredom. Their names were Aholah (*meaning Israel, Ten Tribes*) and Aholibah her sister (*which means Judah, the Jews*). And Aholah (Ten Tribes) played the harlot, and she doted on her lovers, the Assyrians (the people of Nineveh), who were clothed with blue; all of them desirable young men, riding upon horses (*gay and flashy, as the pictures on the walls now show*). She (Ten Tribes) committed whoredom with them. With their idols she defiled herself; wherefore, I have delivered her (Ten Tribes) into the hands of her lovers, the Assyrians; and when her sister (Judah, Jews) saw this she was more corrupt than Israel (Ten Tribes). I saw that they both (Israel and Jews) took one way; for when she (Judah) saw men portrayed upon the wall with vermilion, with girdles upon their loins, in dyed attire, she doted on them. (*Here are the red pictures and carvings on the walls which we are now digging up out of the ruins of Nineveh.*) Therefore, I will raise up thy lovers (the Assyrians) against thee and they shall strip thee out of thy clothes. (*Strip the Jews.*) I will do these things unto thee because thou hast gone whoring after the heathen (Assyrians) and became polluted with their idols. Thou (Judah, Jews) hast walked in the way of thy sister (Israel, Ten Tribes) and thou shalt drink of thy sister's cup, deep and large, and thou (*Jews*) shalt be filled with sorrow and desolation, with the cup of thy sister Samaria (*meaning the cup of Israel, the Ten Tribes*).—Ezekiel 23.

All of this has come true to the very letter, as we now find those old walls with their carvings and red pictures which represented the gay life of the Nineveh people who defiled us (the Ten Tribes of Israel) with their idols and heathen foolishness so that the Lord drove us out of Palestine and had the king of Assyria take us prisoners, and we lost the prophets out of our ranks and the Lord hid His face away from us so that we have been marauding around over the earth over 2500 years and meeting with all kinds of disaster, such as wars, sweeping diseases, plagues, and, finally, the Roman beast stepped onto the earth and began to behead us and lead us into ignorance and darkness, and we have become drunken and debauched and have snakes in our boots and cut and slash and skin and hang each other in a most desperate way. We (the Ten Tribes) are one of the women which Ezekiel was talking about in his lecture, while the Jews were the other woman; and he says that we were sisters, acting the harlot. The Lord took us, the Ten Tribes, into captivity *first*, so that we were gone over 100 years before He took the Jews. He said that the Jews (our sister) could have learned a lesson from us, but that she (the Jews) *would not*, but became more corrupt than *we* were, and that He would make her (the Jews) drink of *our* bitter cup of sorrow and desolation, and even make them *suck* it out and be laughed to scorn and derision.

> Thou (Judah, Jews) hast walked in the way of thy sister Israel (Ten Tribes); therefore, I will give her cup (Ten Tribe cup) into thine hand (*into Jews' hand*). Thou shalt drink it deep and large and *suck it out*, and be laughed to scorn and derision and be filled with sorrow and desolation.—Ezekiel 23:31-34.

How *terribly* true the above has been. Look at the long weary road of our sister (the Jews); how she has been pounded, whipped and driven from place to place and spit upon by all nations, so that *Russia* does not want our sister (the Jews) and it is cow-hiding her; and England does not want her; and Americans, a few years ago, declared that they would not put up at the same hotels where our sister (Jews) were allowed to stop, and this made the hotel-keepers whip our sister out and refuse to

allow her a chair or a bed or a meal. She has had
a desperate and *terrible* time, just as the Lord said in
the above prophecy, that He would make her (the
Jews) drink *our* bitter cup *deep* and *large* and even
suck it out so as to get all of the dregs and bitter
settlings.

> Because thou (*Israel, Ten Tribes, and Judah, Jews*) hast
> forsaken me and cast me behind thy back, therefore, bear
> thy lewdness. With their idols they have committed
> adultery. I (*the Lord*) will bring up a company upon them
> and will give them to be removed and spoiled (*driven all
> over the earth*), and the company shall stone them with
> stones and despatch them with swords (*fight them*) and burn
> up their houses with fire. Thus will I cause lewdness to
> cease out of the land so that all women (*meaning other
> nations*) may be taught not to do after *your* lewdness (*after
> the wicked idol worship that the Ten Tribes and the Jews were
> practicing*). Ye (*Israel and Judah*) shall bear the sins of your
> idols.—Ezekiel 23:35-49.

Yes, and we have borne the sins of our idols most
severely during the last 3500 years or more, so that
human life or age of persons has run down to the
short period of only 33 years, on an average; whereas, the life or age of persons *used* to be as much as
900 years. Tribulation of every sort has struck us
at every turn. Our "sister" (the Jews) *especially* has
caught her stripes and lashes until she is, to-day,
bleeding and a homeless wanderer, as the above
words of the Lord declare that her houses should
be burned with fire and that she (the Jews, our "sister") should be removed and stoned. She could
have learned a lesson from us, the Ten Tribes, as we
were led away captive 721 B. C., while she, our sister
(the Jews) was not taken prisoner until 606 B. C.
(See the diagram of this history in front part of this
book.) But our sister (the Jews) would not learn,
but was more corrupt than were we (see Ezek. 23:11);

therefore, she caught the extreme bitterness in the bottom of our cup and was compelled to suck it dry. It is curious that people will not hear, but rush on to destruction.

How *terribly* true the prophecies are; and they are actual, literal things that have taken place and are yet to occur on *this earth* with people, governments and countries. Here we have a great bundle of predictions all tied together in this one lecture of Ezekiel. We have dug up out of the earth the palaces and temples with their pictures and carvings, about which he talks. We now look back over our long and terrible road of over 2500 years and we can see that we, as one of the women, acted the harlot and have received our dreadful punishment; and we see our sister (*the Jews*), the other woman mentioned by Ezekiel, how she has licked the dust and is to-day thrown out of home and country and is whipped and spit upon because we both (the two sisters) went whoring after those foolish things of the Assyrians, over at Nineveh and Babylon. Of course we had warnings by the prophets who described the road we would have to travel if we did not behave ourselves, but we were *then* just like we are *now*; we did not believe them. We said it "*would not come in our day,*" and that if it ever *did* come it would be away up in the sky, among *spirits*, and that it would never take place on this earth. We looked on that gay city of Nineveh where the king had a palace covering eight acres of ground, with the walls painted with various kinds of scenery; and we saw the huge stone walls around the city which was sixty miles around it, and we looked out on the 1500 towers, 200 feet high, shooting up out of the walls; and we looked through the streets and counted thousands of gay people. We saw the powerful army riding upon horses and decked with flashy trappings; and we gazed with astonishment at the great idol god *Nisroch* which took our eye much more than the spiritual God of Israel; and we thought we were having a hilarious time, never dreaming that the great city would be completely covered over with dirt, and that we would be cast out as wanderers to fight against the elements of destruction, with no God to speak to us. It all came *terribly* true upon us and our sister, the Jews.

The children of Israel shall abide many days without a (inspired) king and without a prince.—Hosea 3:4.

People argued incorrectly *then* just as they are arguing *falsely now*, that it was all symbols, to occur in the sky after death. So it is with the prophecies yet to come to pass. People will not believe that the present governments must go down and a new order of things take the place. They say it is all symbols to occur in the "beyond," but time will show to them their error.

The prophecies say that all the governments of this earth will be thrown down and be blown away like chaff and that the *New and Latter House of Israel* called the Elect will take possession of the earth and rule it. And I know that such a movement of the Lord is now being prepared, and that all things must give way before it, but the inhabitants of the earth toss their heads with a sneer and go on and say that it will "never come in our day," even if it ever comes. They look upon the great capitals of the various nations of earth, and the armies and cannons and the flashy trappings of war generals, and they say these things never will be torn down and buried out of sight. But wait a few years, until the present commotion takes on increased force and all things begin to tremble. But I am not talking about the world coming to an end. Not at all. The outcome of it all, gathered from the Bible, being minutely described in my books Nos. 2 and 3, it will not be discussed here. Suffice it to say, that hundreds and thousands of bricks, tablets, pottery, monuments and cities are being dug up, all over the world, which show that the prophets knew what they were talking about. Some time ago a love-letter was dug up; it was in the form of a brick or a clay slab on which the message had been written while the brick was soft and green, so that when it became dry and hard the message remained. And while this brick love-letter (at first thought) cuts no figure with my subjects being discussed, yet (on *second* thought) it *does* come forward as a witness to prove several important points. It (the brick letter) is very ancient, and, therefore, is a good witness to show that people of those days could write, and, therefore, the slabs, pottery, walls, etc., now being found, are genuine ancient history of occurrences, as many of them deal with the transactions of persons mentioned in the Bible, and accounts on the clay tablets show that the Bible writers stated it correctly, but people of to-day argue that the statements in the Bible could not have been written at the time they pretend to have been for the reason that people of those days could not write, but things are being dug up now which put those theories away forever.

Mr. Edward Glaser has made four exploring tours into Arabia, the last extending from 1892 to 1894, and has made some remarkable discoveries, bringing to light matter that materially confirms many Bible narratives. He demonstrates that the people who inhabited this part of the world were well informed and skilled in the art of writing even before the time of Moses. This is death to the theories advanced by the high critics, who maintain that the art of writing in the time of Moses was not sufficiently advanced to justify the conclusion that Moses really wrote the Pentateuch (the first five books of the Old Testament). And it is now quite evident that Arabia is yet to furnish the proof that will completely refute and overthrow the criticism being directed against the Pentateuch as well as other parts of the Bible. Already these critics feel the ground giving way under them.—*From Messenger.*

Arabia is a large country southeast of Jerusalem. It is supposed to be the native land of Job. It is also thought that the gold for Solomon's Temple was brought from southern Arabia. And it is believed that the Queen of Sheba resided down there about 1000 B. C. She visited Solomon.

It is not generally known that large societies are formed to furnish money and workmen to dig down into the ruins of the ancient cities of Egypt, Assyria and Palestine; and they are bringing to light some astonishments. Only a few months ago Mr. D. L. Miller of the United States was in the city of Jerusalem and watched the work of digging go on, and he writes back to this country a letter about it and from which (with his permission) I clip the following:

We were much interested in the work of excavating the ancient walls, now being carried on by Dr. Bliss, for the Palestine Exploration Fund. We visited the excavations a number of times, climbing down shafts and exploring dark tunnels. At some future time a synopsis of the work done may be given. Here space is only taken for one discovery.

At one point an ancient gate was discovered, and excavating about it, it was found that it occupied the site of not only one, but of two earlier gates. These three gates, one built above the other, are to be seen very plainly. The first thrown down *"sank into the ground,"* as it were, and then a second built above the first and so also the third. We examined all this very carefully and saw the sockets in which the gates swung. The most striking fact about it is that the prophet Jeremiah, speaking of the desolation of Jerusalem, uses this language: "The Lord hath proposed to destroy the wall of the daughter of Zion. . . . *Her gates are sunk in the ground;* he hath destroyed and broken her bars." The sunken gates of the wall of Zion bear testimony in these last days to the truth of the Book of God.—*Mr. Miller's letter.*

Other discoveries are being made which bring us face to face with the hoary past, whose grim witnesses stand up in front of us and look us in the eyes as if to say, "We are messengers sent by the Most High to testify unto the world." People have come and made their tracks and then left the earth, with their lips sealed, but their works leave their history, as is shown by the following:

In the South Pacific Ocean, about 2,000 miles west of South America, and 1,500 miles from the nearest inhabited island, lies the little, heretofore insignificant Easter Island, five by eleven miles in size. Lately some remarkable discoveries were made upon it, consisting of gigantic statues of great antiquity, showing that the island was at one time inhabited by a people far advanced in civilization. No less than 500 of these busts, showing the form of the body from the top of the head to the hips—have been found, varying in size from three to seventy feet in height. The largest one will probably weigh 238,000 tons. These huge busts were moved a considerable distance after they were completed and then skillfully mounted on immense platforms, and now stand as mute witnesses, testifying concerning a wonderful people unknown to the world at this time. On some of the monuments are inscriptions in an unknown language. By and by these inscriptions may be deciphered, then we shall know something of the prehistoric race of this far-away and lonely island. By degrees the old monuments are yielding up their long-kept secrets.—*Messenger.*

Yes, and they throw much light on the Bible. The prophecies have much to say about certain cities and countries and the ruin and desolation that would come upon them for their wrong-doing, and it is now interesting to dig out those things, as they show how *terribly* true the prophets have spoken. It certainly should have some effect to show that the words of those inspired men, thus far, have not failed. Therefore, how can we argue that they will fail when they come to us of *this* day?

In my No. 3 book I have shown by plain calculations that the time is *now* here when a great many of the prophecies will *begin* to come to pass upon us; and when you understand them and what they lay out for us *then* you can see what is causing all of this commotion and uproar over the earth, and it becomes an easy matter to foretell just what the next thing will be and how it will turn. Just now (July, 1896), while I am writing the last lines of this book, with a burning understanding of what is soon to occur on earth, I look out on the people of my country (the United States) and I see them all excited and striving with each other to nominate their favorite candidates for president of the United States, believing that if they can only elect a certain man who advocates a certain *principle* the country will come into a flourishing condition, so that everything will float along nicely; and it is probable that the candidates themselves thoroughly believe that if they can be elected they could bring about a peaceful and prosperous time. All these ideas are an illusion, and time will prove the truth of this statement. The iron hand of prophecy has hold of the lever and it will never stop until it throws down, runs over and grinds into powder and blows away as *chaff* all of the present governments, churches and haughty society. And if those who have a desire to be president of the United

States knew what is hanging over this country their feverish aspirations would cool down into an icy chill, as there is nothing but the most dreadful and terrible trouble in store for them from now until *about* 1915; and whoever shall be holding the office of president during the trembling years *preceding* 1915 will find a greater load on his hands than he can manage, as the Head-Light of the Millennial Kingdom is already in sight, and the rumblings and roarings of its ponderous and dazzling wheels are distinctly heard, but the people and candidates imagine that it is the Tariff after them, and nothing but time will convince them that they are laboring under the mental clouds of insanity, as no human power can prop up the present institutions. It would be throwing a blockade in front of the new order of things, which means that THE NEW AND LATTER HOUSE OF ISRAEL, as described in my book No. 3, will come together within the next few years and push down every thing in front of it and sit down upon the ruins and rule the entire earth with the rod of the Lord which can not be broken; and all things will be compelled to take off their hats and bow to the decree of the Most High, whose well-trained people now being prepared *spiritually* will be as God. The prophecies call them the House of David.

The House of David shall be as God; and I will seek to destroy all the nations that come against Jerusalem. I will smite every horse with astonishment and his rider with madness; and I will make Jerusalem a burdensome stone for all people, and all that burden themselves with it shall be cut in pieces; and Jerusalem shall be inhabited again in her own place.—Zech. 12:3-10.

THE MYSTICAL UNIVERSE.

The Bible writers frequently mention the wonders of the heavens. Their spiritually illuminated minds could see in the arrangement and movements of the planets the marvelous wisdom of God in constructing the machinery of the universe. David, the inspired king over the Israelitish nation, talks about it in this wise:

The heavens declare the glory of God; and the firmament sheweth his handywork. There is no speech nor language where their voice is not heard. Their line is gone out through all the earth, and their words to the end of the world. In them hath he set a tabernacle for the sun.—Psalms 19:1-4.

The writer of Genesis tells us that the planets were made and set in motion to act as a sort of clock-work to measure off time and give *"signs"* and light.

And God said, Let there be lights in the firmament of the heaven to divide the day from the night; and let them be for *signs* and for seasons and for days and years.—Gen. 1:14.

Some of the other inspired men have something to say about these things; therefore, we see that they were attracted by the heavenly machinery which whirls on and on, making seasons and years and marking out time and giving alarms (*"signs"*) and light to the people of this earth.

I claim that all the planets, including this earth, are harnessed together into a great harmonious system like a clock, with some of the wheels running rapidly while others go slowly, and that as the revolutions are completed a change takes place called seasons or years; and that when *all* the wheels come round to their starting point—to the same position (each with the other) as they were at the beginning, a *very great* change occurs, and which may be called an age or a dispensation of God. That is, the world and its inhabitants are turned into a new order of things. And if we understand these movements we can know exactly when the turn is to occur, as the writer of Genesis tells us that they (the planets) are a "sign" to us to warn us that the heavenly clock is about to strike. And it is clear to my mind that this is the situation of things at this time (1896). The planets are making "signs" to us now that the time is almost here when a very great and marvelous change is to take place. I arrive at this conclusion by *several* methods. (1) The prophecies in the Bible declare it. (2) The arrangement of the planets in the heavens "sign" it to us. (3) The general signs of the times point to it. (4) We know that the 2,520 years of Gentile Times are almost expired. But you will ask, How can the planets give us any "sign" that a terrible disturbance is about ready to break loose in the universe? Well, you remember I have shown that the writer of Genesis declares that God made the planets for "signs" and for seasons, etc.; and if they are linked or grouped together into a piece of heavenly clock-work, we know by looking at their positions just how far on their journey they have gone and what condition of atmosphere they produce when they are at a certain point. No one will dispute this, as every one knows that the blustery and icy season comes and remains a while and then disappears, and the warm growing season takes the place. We know just when to look for these seasons. When our position comes to a certain point in the heavenly clock we know what to expect; therefore, the planets and their positions give us a "sign." We have also learned that when great disturbances are occurring among the planets in the heavens, sweeping disaster strikes this earth. Sometimes it is a ravaging disease, while at other times it is a great earthquake, or terrible and destructive floods, or extreme heat and drouth, or general wars among the nations. Do I mean to say that disturbance among the planets in the heavens will throw the nations of this earth into wars? Well, I shall not state it in exactly those words, but I *do* say that astronomers declare it as a fact that when there is a general war among the nations there is also, *at the same time*, a great display or upheaval among the planets in the heavens. You can draw your own conclusions; but you must remember that the New Testament tells us that *"we wrestle not with flesh and blood, but with powers and principalities"* (in the air). That is, some unseen power or *powers* operate over us and throw us into convulsions of some kind, and, as I have before stated, those convulsions are sweeping diseases, earthquakes, floods, drouths and wars. Whatever the causes may be, we know that this earth is influenced by *conditions* and *positions* of other planets, and those who understand these things can calculate many years ahead as to when a great earthquake will occur. Some years ago a scientific gentleman declared that at a certain time in a certain year (five years ahead) an earthquake would occur, followed· by a *terrible* convulsion or eruption of a volcano in Mexico. It occurred just at the time and place as predicted by him. He did not claim to be a prophet by direct inspiration. He based his statement on what he knew about the forces that would be exerted among the planets at a certain time; and as this earth is closely associated with the movements of other heavenly bodies, its actions will be decidedly influenced by them. This being the case, it becomes an easy matter then to ascertain just when to expect disturbances.

Astronomers tell us that from the 9th to the 26th of December, 1901, the planets will all be in a straight line, but that all of them except the earth will be on one side of the sun, leaving the earth (alone) on the other side. Astronomers claim that this was their position at the time of Noah's Flood. Dr. F. M. Close, ex-president of the Tacoma Academy of Science, talks on this as follows:

The Babylonian Tablets are a set of inscribed plates written thousands of years before the Christian era. In these is given an account of the Noachian deluge. These tablets were exhumed from the ancient city of Nineveh and are now in the British Museum at London. They state that Capricornus was the ruling sign of the zodiac at the time of the deluge. Berosus, a Chaldean astronomer, wrote the history of Babylon, and quoted the Babylonian Tablets, and he further declared that when the sun and planets again together occupy the sign of Capricornus another world flood would happen. It is proper to here say that the term "flood" or "deluge" does not mean the end of the world, nor the total extinction of life upon the globe, but the subsidence or sinking of a great body of land, such as a continent, beneath the waters of the ocean. Just now the planets are rapidly approaching that position in which the earth will be on one side of the sun and all the rest of the planets on the other, all ranged in nearly a straight line.—*Dr. Close in a California paper.*

Dr. Close does not think that another flood will be produced, but he is positive that the greatest disturbances that have struck this earth for hundreds of years will be the result. He further says:

The late seismic disturbance, which extended over the Middle and Southeastern States, was one of the preliminary throes of a great cataclysm, the culmination of which may not occur for several years.—*Dr. Close.*

We already notice very great and *terrible* disturbances in the atmosphere. Cyclones, floods, frosts, extreme heat, sweeping winds and drouths are becoming common. They are simply the forerunners, which are coming ahead of the general and *awful* upheaval which is bound to come within a few years. A great combination of things is forming into line. As just stated, the planets come into this peculiar straight-line position, in which all of them will combine their forces and pull against the earth, in 1901. But just before this—viz., 1899—the earth will run into a bee-hive of comets, which come around to us or we come to them every thirty-three years. Professor Falb lectured in Berlin, Germany, on this subject as follows:

That on the 13th of November, 1899, the comet will cut the path of the earth at the point where the earth arrives every year on that date. Even should a collision take place, the material of the comet is so light that no harm would result to the earth, unless the carbonic gas, of which probably all comets consist, should poison the atmosphere. But it is certain that between 2 and 3 a. m. on the 13th of November, 1899, the most awful spectacle of shooting stars will take place that the world has ever witnessed!—*Prof. Falb.*

It will well pay the people of this country to sit up all night to see the great display in the heavens. It will occur sometime between the 13 and the 15th of November, 1899. This is so near to the 1901 disturbance that the two will be more or less combined in action and, added to other things, will make this earth heave and roll in more ways than one. The atmosphere will be so greatly disturbed that a variety of things is liable to occur. Earthquakes are almost *certain* to be *one* kind of the trouble, with sweeping diseases (*especially* those affecting the brain and nerves), cyclones, floods and drouths and, probably, *extreme* heat are in the line of probabilities and may be expected. As to the heat, scientific men are almost certain that it will come, for the reason that the earth will be in the right position to get it. Passing through the shower of blazing comets will be *one* cause of increased heat, with other causes to be added. As to this, Professor Proctor, the astronomer, uses this language:

> In about 1897-8 the heat of the sun will be so enormously increased by the impact of a comet as to destroy life upon this earth.—*Prof. Proctor, the astronomer.*

This earth is *already* coming into the *edge* of these disastrous things so that cyclones, drouths, floods, heat and peculiar whirls in the atmosphere are common occurrences. Only a few weeks ago the Pacific Ocean rose up out of its bed and ran out on the dry land and destroyed thirty thousand people in five minutes, according to newspaper accounts, which I clip as follows:

THIRTY THOUSAND VICTIMS.
Entire Towns Wiped Out of Existence by a Tidal Wave Which Gave No Warning.

On the 15th of June, at 8:30 o'clock in the evening, a seismic wave struck the northeast coast of the main land (Japan), throughout a distance of about 200 miles, and in five minutes 30,000 people were killed and 12,000 houses destroyed. So stupendous was the atmospheric disturbance that it not only leveled forests to the ground, but also stripped the trees of bark and twigs, reducing them to blanched skeletons. Corpses recovered within a few hours of death looked as though they had undergone a week's decomposition. The wounds suffered by the survivors and shown by the bodies of the dead are also of a shocking description. In some cases the flesh is torn into shreds, exposing the bones beneath; in others the eyes are forced out of their sockets; in others the trunks seem to have been wrenched asunder by forces acting in opposite directions; in others the skin looks as though it had been plunged in boiling water. Such are the details of death and ruin, the terrible totals at this moment of writing being 29,073 killed, 7,737 wounded and 7,844 houses washed away or wrecked.—*Daily papers' report.*

While the above mentioned disaster was yet fresh in our minds another unusual and dreadful thing struck this earth with a roar and blazing heat that frightened the inhabitants.

Tucson, Ariz., Aug. 17, 1896.—An immense meteor struck the desert about two miles north of Hall's ranch. The concussion was terrible. Cupboards were upset, dishes were thrown on the floor and the house trembled as a leaf. The noise was like that of many cannon fired simultaneously. The air for miles around was filled with sulphurous gas, and the meteor came down red and smoking. It covers about two acres of ground, appearing to be imbedded hundreds of feet in the earth, and now forms a great mound in the desert. A herder's hut and corral were in the meteor's path. The herder, his wife and three children, together with about 1,200 sheep, went down under the mighty mass. A large party left here yesterday evening to view the wonder and to get further particulars. It is about 60 miles north of Tucson.—*Newspaper account.*

Some time ago an earthquake ran through or under the sea and upset an island on which a city was built. The whole city was tilted off into the water *instantly* as though it were a fly on a cart wheel. It is curious that people do not notice the unusual frequency of destructive earthquakes nowadays. Scarcely any one seems to see the daily papers' reports of them. All these things are simply the *beginning* or *edge* of the disasters which will soon strike this earth and make it heave and wabble like a ship in a storm; and the combined forces operating against the earth will finally throw it clear out of its present orbit or track and *may*, probably, land it into another system of planets with another sun as their center. I say it *may* do this. I do not say that it will. This, of course, will change the climatic conditions around this earth, but while it is passing from its present orbit to its new position it will, probably, lose *part* of the light of *this* sun so that the light will be grayish or yellow. It seems that this will occur while the earth and the other planets are changing their positions.

And it shall come to pass in that day, that the light shall not be clear nor dark, but it shall be one day which shall be known to the Lord, not day nor night; but it shall come to pass that at evening time it shall be light. And it shall be in that day that living waters shall go out from Jerusalem, half of them toward the former sea and half of them toward the hinder sea, and the Lord shall be king over all the earth. In that day there shall be one Lord and his name one.—Zech. 14:6-9.

Thus we see that there is to be a very great disturbance among the planets of the heavens, so that the light of this sun will not be what it is *now* to us. The change will produce a new condition in the sun and moon.

The light of the moon shall be as the light of the sun and the light of the sun shall be sevenfold, as the light of seven days, in the day that the Lord bindeth up the breach of his people and healeth the stroke of their wound. Behold the name of the Lord cometh from far, burning with his anger, and the burden thereof is heavy; his lips are full of indignation and his tongue as a devouring fire, and his breath, as an overflowing stream, shall reach to the midst of the neck, to sift the nations. And the Lord shall cause his glorious voice to be heard and shall shew the lighting down of his arm, and with the flame of a devouring fire, with scattering and tempest and hailstones.—Isa. 30:26-31.

The above scripture confirms what I have been saying about the extraordinary position of the planets, and about the earth moving out of its place and going to some new location.

> The earth shall reel to and fro like a drunkard and shall be *removed like a cottage;* and the transgression thereof shall be heavy upon it. And it shall come to pass in that day that the Lord shall punish the host of the high ones, and the kings of the earth upon the earth, and they shall be gathered together as prisoners are gathered. Then the moon shall be confounded and the sun ashamed when the Lord of hosts shall reign in Mount Zion, and in Jerusalem, and before his ancients (*the Royal Body of Priests, called the Elect*).—Isa. 24:20-23. I will shake the heavens, and *the earth shall remove out of her place,* for the stars of heaven and the constellations thereof shall not give their light, and the sun shall be darkened *in his going forth,* and the moon shall not cause her light to shine; and I will punish the world for their evil and the wicked for their iniquity and I will cause the arrogancy of the proud to cease and will lay low the haughtiness of the terrible.—Isa. 13:6-14. And there shall be *signs in the sun and in the moon and in the stars,* and upon the earth distress of nations, with perplexity; the sea and the waves roaring, for the powers of heaven shall be shaken.—Luke 21:25-26. And it shall come to pass in that day, saith the Lord, that I will cause the sun to go down at noon, and I will darken the earth in the clear day, and I will turn your feasts into mourning, and I will make it as the mourning of an only son, and the end thereof as a bitter day.—Amos 8:9-10.

Thus we see that the Bible writers were not afraid to talk about astronomy and the movements of the planets in the heavens, for the reason that they knew of the great disturbance that would be due at the end of this age, and this goes to confirm what I have heretofore stated, that the planets were all yoked together into one great clock-work to measure off time in God's dispensations and give us a *"sign"* as to when the heavenly time-piece would strike; and I declare it that the alarm is already jingling, but the world is arrogant and proud and refuses to hear, notwithstanding the fact that these disturbances are already commencing, and they will overtake us bitterly within a few years. But I am aware of the fact that nothing but time will convince people of the truth of these statements. Political, social and religious matters are already disrupted and beyond the hope of reconstruction, and yet, in the face of this we see the people of this country (United States) talking about the Tariff, Sound Money, Free Coinage, and a host of other notions that can have no effect *whatever* on bringing about a peaceful condition. The Lord's dispensations will change whether Congress does or does not consent. And during the change a *terrible* upheaval will occur and it will not stop to ask Congress any thing about it. It is already striking and Congress is powerless to remedy it.

> The day of the Lord cometh as a thief in the night, for when they shall say, Peace and safety, then sudden destruction cometh upon them, and they shall not escape.—1 Thes. 5:1-4.

In the face of all this and the present signs of the times it *does* seem ridiculous to see people running around arguing that the election of a certain man or men and the enacting of certain laws by Congress will bring us peace and prosperity.

I argue this case from what is *called* the scientific standpoint, for the reason that most people declare that the prophecies are not reliable and, therefore, they cannot be depended upon to give us a correct statement of what is to occur. But I know positively that these notions of the people about the prophecies are not correct, as I have investigated ancient history and have compared it with the statements of the prophets and I find that things have come to pass *exactly* as they predicted they would. Therefore, it is reasonable to think that the things *yet* to come to pass will take place exactly as stated by the prophets. As for myself, it is not necessary to go over the *so-called* scientific part of this argument and examine the position and condition of the planets in order to convince my mind that some terrible and dreadful disturbances will take place on this earth in the near future, as I am *already* convinced that the prophets understood their business and foresaw (by inspiration) the occurrences as they will take place, and I have quoted to you some of their words in order that you may see that they entirely agree with the statements of what are *called* scientific men of to-day. I have shown to you that they say that very great and terrible heat is *liable* to strike this earth in the near future, and this is in perfect harmony with the statements of the New Testament writers.

But the heavens and the earth which are now kept in store, reserved unto fire against the day of judgment and perdition of ungodly men. The day of the Lord will come as a thief in the night, in the which the heavens shall pass away with a great noise and the elements shall melt with fervent heat.—2 Peter 3:7-12.

It is proper to call your attention to the fact that the great disturbance among the planets will be accompanied by a terrible upheaval among men on this earth, so that the angry and distressed condition of the people added to the heat produced from *seemingly* natural causes will make the fiery elements so extremely severe on human life that a very great proportion of the inhabitants of this earth will perish. Only those who shall endure unto the end shall be saved. The *time* when these disturbances will occur is calculated and set forth plainly in my No. 3 book, which shows that it will occur between 1896 and 1915, but no special year is set. It is enough to know that it is within eighteen years.

The theory that the planetary condition will produce heat so great as to destroy things seems to be confirmed by the words of St. John:

> The first angel sounded and there followed hail and fire mingled with blood, and they were cast upon the earth; and the third part of trees was burnt up; and all green grass was burnt up; and the third part of the creatures which were in the sea and had life, died; and the third part of the ships were destroyed.—Rev. 8:7-9.

It is useless to carry the argument farther. I have shown sufficient to convince anyone (who is willing to be convinced) that we are coming to a time of tribulation and sorrow the like of which the world has never seen, and they will be upon us before the general public is aware of it, as people are *now* just as they were in the days of Noah. They will neither heed nor believe, although the signs are coming thick and fast, but the world seems not to notice these things. People are too busily engaged in stealing from each other and running after dollars and sexual matters to think much about the roaring cyclones, the rumbling earthquakes, the heavings of the sea, the falling of red-hot monster meteors, the disrupted condition of governments, the alarming increase of insanity, the floods and drouths walking hand in hand, the *total* ungodliness of the churches, the devilishness of society, which is as rotten and putrid as hell itself, the extreme pride and haughtiness of men and women, their bitter hatred towards any thing spiritual, and the flippant indignation they show towards those who are calling the world's attention to the great change soon to occur. All these things are right before our eyes *now*, and the bugle is sounding, and God is mustering the hosts to the great day of the battle of God Almighty, and yet the world jogs along, seemingly unconscious of the uprising now taking place. Most of those who *do* see it imagine that *Congress* can settle it. This is absurdity gone to seed, and those who hold to the idea are just as much in the dark as those who do not see the disrupted condition *at all*. They are *all* blind together.

Our Near Future.

THE TURNS AND CHANGES TO OCCUR IN SOCIETY, GOVERNMENTS AND CHURCHES DURING THE 20 YEARS FROM 1896 CAREFULLY SET FORTH. NEW AND INTERESTING. OTHER TALKS ON OTHER SUBJECTS.

Redding's Millennial Kingdom book having been hailed by the public with such universal delight on account of its new and interesting ideas, the author of it has written other books on interesting subjects —making a list as follows:

No. 1. Doctors and Medicines... .. .. 5c
No. 2. The Millennial Kingdom... .. .. 50c
No. 3. Our Near Future... .. .. 50c
No. 4. The Vaccination Curse... .. .. 10c
No. 5. Curious Causes... .. .. 20c
No. 6. That Woman Question... .. .. 10c
No. 7. The Three Churches.................15c
No. 8. The Rifting Wedge....................10c
No. 9. Mysteries Unveiled... .. .. 50c

No. 1, DOCTORS AND MEDICINE, is a *small* booklet containing quotations from the leading physicians of the world showing that medicine is a humbug and that it destroys many people instead of helping them. Price, 5 cts. each.

No. 2, THE MILLENNIAL KINGDOM, shows that we Americans are the Lost Ten Tribes of Israel and are to rise to high spiritual light and lead the world in the Millennial Kingdom ON EARTH 1,000 years. Death will cease. People will live hundreds of years, like a tree (Isaiah 65:20-22). Its preparation is causing present commotion. It does not advocate that the world is coming to an end and be burned up with fire, or anything of the kind, but that our most glorious time on earth is soon to set in, and that sickness and death will cease, and that the present wicked way will be given up to a better and more godly life. It shows that resurrections are going on *now*. It shows so many interesting and instructive things and is so entirely different from other books heretofore published on Millennial subjects that a description of it cannot be given; it must be read to be known, as the subjects are numerous and plainly stated, and the print is large and clear. Many letters from those who have read it declare that it is the most interesting and entertaining book they ever saw. Here is a sample of the way they write about it:

Gurdon, Ark., Jan. 2, '95.
Your book is ahead of anything I ever read. It is being loaned out all the time and everyone likes it. You ought to have an agent here; it would sell faster than hot cakes.
Mary E. Ryan.

Hallowell, Kans., Oct. 22, '94.
Yours is one of the grandest books I ever read. I can't praise it enough. My husband thinks it the best book he

ever read, too. I do all I can to get people to send for it and I loan my book out to all. E. Lamasters.

Moody, Mo., November 17, 1894.
I do most heartily recommend your book. If men will only read it, each one will receive additional knowledge of more than ordinary merit. Dr. J. Ashworth.

Columbus, Texas, Oct. 13, '94.
The book came and I read it with much interest. It is the best and plainest interpretation of the Bible I ever read; the facts are too plain to be mistaken. I wish every Christian in the land could read it. Send me fifteen for $5.00.
B. Gay.

Sanborn, North Dakota, Dec. 21, '94.
Your book is a good one. What can you let me have them for by the dozen? D. F. Siegfried.

It is as interesting as a romance, and every old petrified fossil should read it and awake to some idea of the times we are living in. M. J. Clarkson, Melrose, Mass.

Richmond, Ind., November 23, 1894.
I have read your book with much interest. It is a book ahead of the times in which we live. G. W. Pinnick.

You should read this book. It will help you understand some of the mysteries of the Bible. Price, bound in paper cover, 50 cts.; cloth, $1.

No. 3, OUR NEAR FUTURE, shows so many interesting things which everybody should know that a description of it cannot be given without setting out the whole book. It shows that the world went under a cloud of darkness at a certain time for a purpose and that it is about to come out from under it. It unravels and removes the veil from the wonderful and fateful dreams mentioned in the 2d and 4th chapters of Daniel. They were a foreshadowing of certain great movements which were to occur on earth, and this No. 3 book shows that the latter part of them is just now *beginning* to come to pass. It shows what the result will be and how it will affect the governments, churches and society. It shows who the Turks are and what figure they cut in the great changes which are soon to occur; and why they hold the center of all the nations; and why the Armenian trouble started up and what the result will be and how it will change various governments. It shows that a new nation is quietly forming to occupy the central position of all the earth and rule with a rod of iron and break down all other governments; and that this is the sole cause of the present upheaval everywhere. It shows that the iron band is about to be removed from the stump, as mentioned in Daniel 4:10-16. This is a curious mystery which the No. 3 book brings to light. Also unveils the great image seen in the King's Dream, Dan. 2:31-46.

It contains a minute description of how governments and society will turn within 20 years from 1896, and sets forth the reasons for such prediction with such clearness that not many persons will even *attempt* to dispute it. It is not founded on guesswork, like most of such predictions heretofore have been. Its statements are supported with such a *quality* of proof that even a skeptic public will not sneer. It does not advocate that the world is coming to an end and be burned up, but just the reverse. It shows that our grandest time on earth is to come yet, but that a season of trouble must precede it. Those who are not acquainted with the subject will be surprised at the vast amount of new proof set forth in the book. The general public does not know that many discoveries and unearthing of things have occurred in recent years to throw light on these subjects. The signs of the times support the statements in the book. Price, paper cover, 50 cts.; cloth, $1.

No. 4, THE VACCINATION CURSE, shows how the human race is being polluted with leprosy, syphilis, catarrh, consumption, blindness, deafness and a great host of destructive diseases by vaccination; and that the statistics of England show a greater number of deaths from small-pox among vaccinated people than those *not* vaccinated, besides the crippling, killing and ruining of persons *direct* by vaccination. It is a horrible devil walking over the earth sticking poison into the innocent. Unscrupulous persons in large cities gather up a quantity of pus from persons dying with syphilis and other private diseases and send it out all over the world to make money out of it. Every person should have his eyes opened on this *awful* subject and stand against the enacting of compulsory vaccination laws. No time to lose, as the legislatures are trying to force us by laws to have syphilis and other deadly diseases stuck into us. This curse struck the earth like a withering blast, years ago, and the race is now reaping what it sowed. Price, 10 cts. each; 12 for $1; 27 for $2; 70 for $5.

No. 5, CURIOUS CAUSES, shows an astonishing collection of facts about the powerful unseen mental and spiritual laws, which operate on humanity unawares and produce disaster and destruction or bring rich rewards, just according to the way they are handled. It shows *especially* how terrible or how grand these laws can be made operate on unborn children if the mother understands how to turn them to advantage. She can and *does* make her unborn child a vicious murderer by her own thoughts or she can make it moral and lovely. This is no idle tale; the book shows this with evidence beyond dispute. Every person should keep a supply of these books and make a special effort to put one in the hand of every man, woman and child and thereby open the people's eyes on these unseen causes, which are producing so much disaster. No parent wants to bring forth a child to be a liar, thief, robber, murderer or cruel in any way; and yet ignorance of these unseen but powerful laws is doing just this thing. The facts set out in it *must* convince you that this subject is a wide field and needs *every* body as *workers* to go from house to house with these little books, and *especially* put them in the hands of young girls, from 10 years old up to 110, so that their minds will have a clear knowledge of these unseen laws before trash and vicious things fill their heads. It is the teaching that is impressed on us while young that stays with us through life. Do not be afraid to let your *children* understand these things; sooner the better, so that their morbid curiosity about birth and all sex matters will not run away with them. Be sure to have them know that their bad thoughts will imprint bad things on their own bodies and on the bodies and minds of their children just the same as birth-marks are imprinted. This is why very young girls should read the little book, No. 5; and it is your solemn duty to *spread* the proven facts set out in it. It is small and cheap and the facts are put in a clear, simple way. Order 50 or 100 and then watch your chances to mention it, and nearly every person will spend twenty cents for one if you will have the book *right ready* to hand over, *then and there.* Every dry goods store, post office, barber shop, cigar store, restaurant, milliner shop, hotel, and news stand should have on sale, in their show cases, a quantity of these booklets. The subject is important and affects the whole human family. Price, 20 cts. each; 6 for $1; 13 for $2; 35 for $5.00.

No. 6, THAT WOMAN QUESTION, discusses *briefly* the political and social movement being agitated by women, and calls their attention to some things which the world is viewing *quietly* but *seriously*. It points out some of the mistakes women are making at this time when their cause is being agitated, and what the final result will be if they do not change their ways. There are some prophecies in the Bible for them, and also against them, under certain conditions. They should know what these are. Price of this No. 6 booklet, 10 cts. each; 12 for $1; 30 for $2; 100 for $5.

No. 7, THE THREE CHURCHES, shows what the Bible says about the three kinds of people, who would be on the earth at these times and that each would call themselves by a name; and that only *one* of them would be the real Church of God. This No. 7 booklet shows who these three are and that the third one is just now forming into the real Church, which the New Testament calls the *Elect*, which are to be picked out and to overcome death and rule the earth 1,000 years. Isaiah 65:20-22. But these three churches are not any three of the denominations now calling themselves churches. It is an *entirely* different dividing of the world into three groups named in the booklet. This is a curious fact which most persons will see and admit after reading this No. 7, as it shows that the prophecy has come true to the very letter and that the third group is to be the adopted or *sent* church, built by the Lord and the gates of hell will not prevail against it, just as Jesus declares in Matt. 16:18. The various denominations now on earth will look at this Bible talk with a new understanding as to which church is right, and which is the recognized church by the Lord. This has agitated their minds a long time, and this booklet will give them something about which to think, and show to them what the Bible says about the *real* church, which is just now forming as the Elect. But it has no reference to any new sect or organization now forming, as there are many of such. It is an entirely different thing. The No. 7 booklet shows what various words in our English Bible mean in the Hebrew and the Greek languages, from which our English translation came. A failure to understand this change in the meaning by translating has caused many false ideas about Bible doctrines. Take the words *"everlasting,"* *"forever,"* *"world,"* *"grave,"* *"hell"* and many others for instances. The booklet does not enter into a discussion about *all* these words, but shows by only a *few* how entirely different the ancient language meaning was from our English meaning nowadays. No arguments. Simply brief showings. You should read it. Price, 15 cts. each; 8 for $1; 50 for $5.

No. 8, THE RIFTING WEDGE, shows that gold will be the bone of contention over which the world will snarl and strive, and that it will finally grind the nations to pieces so that the kingdoms of this world will become the kingdom of the spiritual Christ. In other words, the *money* question is an instrument to bring on the destruction of the nations as governments, for the reason that money is said to be the root of all evil. People make it their god and worship it and rely upon it, and the God of Israel will *permit* it to rule tyrannically over the people and grind them down so that they can see its destructive character. They are already feeling its iron grip, and this little No. 8 booklet shows by Bible prophecy and other things what the final outcome of it will be, and that the New Age, which will set in *about* 1915, will overthrow this god of the world (money) and put exchange on an entirely different basis, which politicians do not understand. They should read this booklet, not that it discusses all the long tedious points of *"finance,"* but it cuts straight across and comes to the vital point at once and shows what the result of the present gold agitation will be. Price, 10 cts. each; 12 for $1; 100 for $5.

No. 9, MYSTERIES UNVEILED, is what *some* people would call startling on account of the many unearthings and bringing forth of things long hidden out of sight of the general world. It shows God's plan of the ages by the little halls and rooms built in the stone pyramid of Egypt 4,000 years ago. Their lengths, slants and turns let the secret out (1 inch to a year). No wonder the prophets said that God has wonders in Egypt. (See Isaiah 19:19-20 and Jer. 32:20.) The halls, length and turns are shown. Also contains an accurate account of the recent finding of the preserved body of Pharaoh, with his name (Rameses) written on his breast, after his death, 3,300 years ago; photograph of him is set in book. Also shows the wonderful lessons to be learned from the Golden Ark of the Covenant, which is hidden away, probably, for future discovery. Also unveils the mysteries of the book of Revelation and shows who the great Scarlet Woman is, as mentioned by St. John, and what she has done on earth, and that her number is 666, just as stated in Rev. 13:18. The showing of this number (666) is made clear by an astonishing discovery, and a picture of the head *man* in the mystery is set forth in book. The book further shows the source from which we got our color, called *cardinal red;* and that it has something to do with Bible prophecy. Also shows who Napoleon was and what he was born for and why he was so successful up to a certain date and then collapsed suddenly. Shows the wonderful ear-mark which God placed on the Great Seal of the United States to brand us as the Lost Tribes of Jacob. Picture of seal is set in book so that every man can see the mark or design made to brand us as *the* people who were driven out of Palestine 721 B. C. This information *alone* is worth many times the price of the book, as it shows that the mighty God is watching over us for a purpose, which purpose is fully set forth in the No. 3 book entitled OUR NEAR FUTURE; and those who read No. 9 should also read Nos. 2 and 3, in which the different branches of the subject are carried. Some wonderful things will occur on this earth within the next 20 years, and these three books, Nos. 2, 3 and 9, discuss them in a new and plain way and show conclusively that the idea which the people have about the manner of the coming of the Christ and the world coming to an end is *all* wrong, and that the teaching by men the last one hundred years on this subject, has been misleading. It shows where the Garden of Eden was located and that it was an actual fact on earth. The location and the rivers mentioned in the Bible about it are pointed out so clearly that people will be astonished at finding that the long mysterious Garden spot was really on this earth. Price of No. 9, paper cover, 50 cts.; cloth, $1.

All of the above described books are written by the same author (W. A. Redding). Always write your name and address *plainly* and *state your county sure* and write out in *full* the names of the books you want. Do not undertake to order just by the number, as sometimes your figures are not written plainly and you are liable to get the wrong book. Two-cent postage stamps taken as pay, but send cash if convenient.

Address the author,

W. A. REDDING,

Navarre,

Dickinson Co., Kansas.

A

OTHER HELPS.

Realizing the fact that God is uncovering to men the secrets of the dark past, which enable us to understand the mysterious sayings of the Bible, I have selected from other authors a list of valuable books which every person should read. You should not remain ignorant of these great subjects with a combination of good things lying within your reach. I will, therefore, furnish at the following listed price, these carefully selected books. (I pay postage).

DICTIONARY OF THE BIBLE.—Revised in the light of recent researches in Bible lands. Over 200,000 copies have been sold. New, clear type. Good paper. 360 pictures. Strongly bound, and is an invaluable help to all persons. Its 18 maps are from the latest authorities, and are printed in colors. 720 pages. Outside measures 6¼ by 9 inches. Nearly 2 inches thick. Cloth, $2. Sheep, $2.50.

This is a highly valuable book for every body. The 360 pictures alone will give you ideas which you never could get from reading. This book tells you all about the ups and downs and ancient history of Jerusalem and of Babylon and all those ancient Bible lands and cities and men and things generally. When you read in the Bible about a certain thing, turn to this history and it will tell you all about it. In fact, this great book is a whole library condensed and put into one book and arranged alphabetically so that you can turn to it quickly. You should have it by all means.

CRUDEN'S CONCORDANCE.—561 pages. Clear type. Cloth, $1.25.

SACRED GEOGRAPHY AND ANTIQUITIES.—By Prof. E. P. Barrows, D. D. In this faithfully prepared volume the scholar will find the most important information on all the topics included under the title furnished by the large and costly works of the best and latest scholars. Palestine and all Bible lands are minutely described: the domestic institutions and customs of the Jews, their dress, agriculture, sciences, and arts; their forms of government, justice, and military affairs; their temple services, priesthood, sacrifices, and religious customs. Five maps and numerous engravings. 685 pages. Cloth, $2.50.

THE STORY OF THE BIBLE, by Charles Foster. Everybody should have this book. Easy to understand. The pictures alone are worth the price of the book, as they impress the mind with the scenes and incidents narrated in the Bible. It gives you a clear understanding of things. 500,000 sold. Size, 6¾ by 8¾. 704 pages. 300 pictures. It is of absorbing interest. Thrilling incidents of Bible history, told in easy language. Cloth, $1.75.

BIBLE PICTURES AND WHAT THEY TEACH US, by Charles Foster. Containing 315 illustrations of Old and New Testament scenes, with short descriptions. They make lasting impressions on the mind. Pages 8 x 10 inches, each containing one or more pictures. Over 150,000 copies of this popular book have already been sold. It is needed in every house where there are children, and is useful, also, to older persons who desire a pictorial Bible history. Price, $1.50.

THE BIBLE HISTORY, by Alfred Edersheim. 7 vols., cloth, each $1.00; the set in a neat box, $7.00.
1. The World Before the Flood, and History of the Patriarchs.
2. The Exodus and Wanderings in the Wilderness.
3. Israel in Canaan under Joshua and the Judges.
4. Israel under Samuel, Saul and David, to the Birth of Solomon.
5. Israel and Judah from the Birth of Solomon to the Reign of Ahab.
6. Israel and Judah from Ahab to the Decline of the two Kingdoms.
7. Israel and Judah from the Decline of the two Kingdoms to the Assyrian and Babylonian Captivity. Containing full Scripture References and Subject Indexes to the whole series.

THE LOST TRIBES OF ISRAEL, or *Europe and America in History and in Prophecy*, by Prof. C. L. McCartha, is a book of 210 pages, which every person should read.

The author starts at the beginning of things and *briefly* runs along through the various nations and shows how the Divine Hand has turned and divided the governments to suit the one great purpose of perfecting the human race; and he finally ends with the United States of America, as the place where the climax of the work is to take place. This is exactly what I (Redding) am trying to make the people see in my *own* publications, which were written long before I ever heard of this book of Prof. McCartha's. It is a fact that whoever studies the Lost Ten Tribes of Israel subject will arrive at this same conclusion without ever examining other men's works. It is the hidden subject of this earth and upon it hangs the world's great change, which is now commencing and whirling society, governments and churches into one great upheaval, which will finally come to a focus in the greatest trouble the world has ever seen, with a chosen Elect Israel sitting on top of the ruins ruling the world religiously, politically and socially. It is impossible for one to understand the Bible and its great theme without understanding this Ten Tribes subject. You might as well try to learn Arithmetic with multiplication, addition and subtraction left out. This is one of the reasons why Bible teaching (at present) is so woefully mixed up. Preachers and church people (as a class) know nothing of this subject and, therefore, they have things turned around and the Bible thrown out of square, and they think Israel means Jews. When ordering this book from me, be careful to state that it is Prof. McCartha's book you want, so as to distinguish it from my own publications on Israel. Price of McCartha's book, paper, 75c.; cloth, $1.

THE MISSING LINKS, or *The Anglo-Saxons the Ten Tribes of Israel*, by Morton W. Spencer. 1,000 historical and prophetical proofs of our Hebrew-Saxon ancestry. Being a history of our Saxon race from the "call" of Abraham, showing the ONE plan of redemption. America and England the foci of this dispensation. Christ the center of all the ages. The key to our success. The lion's share in the future glory, and what shall come of it. Search and marvel. About 500 pages. Price, $2.00.

Always write plainly the name of the book you want. I pay postage. Stamps taken, but send cash if convenient.

W. A. REDDING,

Navarre,

Dickinson Co., Kansas.

THE TRIBES is a monthly paper advocating that we, the Anglo-Saxons, are the Lost Ten Tribes of Israel, who left Palestine 721 B. C., and that we are to lead the world. It throws light on the turns and whirls of the various nations as they occur and points out the prophecy regarding them. It is the only paper of this kind published in the United States and should be in every home. It is published by an association scattered all over America, with headquarters in Denver, Colorado. The best historians and students of prophecy in this country write for its columns. Subscription, 50 cts. a year. Address *The Tribes*, Denver, Colorado.

THE CAYSTER is a small *monthly* leaflet claiming that Christ is now present and that the great tribulation is begun. It aims to note the turns things are taking and give its interpretation of the Scriptures. Subscription, 25 cts. a year. Samples free. Address Geo. P. Pierce, Deshler, Henry Co., Ohio.

THE SQUARE WORLD is a small monthly paper advocating that the world is square and not round. The editor sells a large map showing what he conceives to be the truth about the world and the movements of the sun and moon. He explains how it is that people *think* they go round the world but do not. He is cow-hiding astronomers and is *really* knocking out some of their firmly accepted theories. He is also lashing the churches with a keen switch and points them to Christ as the only church worth knowing anything about. If he can knock out any false theories in astronomy, theology or any other ology, let him go ahead, as the world has come to a point where all false doctrines must go down, and whoever whets his butcher-knife and starts out after them has my consent. Subscription for *Square World*, 50 cts. a year. Address it at Hot Springs, South Dakota.

www.ingramcontent.com/pod-product-compliance
Lightning Source LLC
Chambersburg PA
CBHW020829230426
43666CB00007B/1157